T0146598

Anya's Story

Anya's Story

You Are Not Alone

HILDA JOURNEY

ANYA'S STORY
YOU ARE NOT ALONE

iUniverse books may be ordered through booksellers or by contacting:

iUniverse
1663 Liberty Drive
Bloomington, IN 47403
www.iuniverse.com
1-800-Authors (1-800-288-4677)

Because of the dynamic nature of the Internet, any web addresses or links contained in this book may have changed since publication and may no longer be valid. The views expressed in this work are solely those of the author and do not necessarily reflect the views of the publisher, and the publisher hereby disclaims any responsibility for them.

Any people depicted in stock imagery provided by Thinkstock are models, and such images are being used for illustrative purposes only. Certain stock imagery © Thinkstock.

ISBN: 978-1-5320-3586-9 (sc)
ISBN: 978-1-5320-3585-2 (e)

Library of Congress Control Number: 2017916739

Print information available on the last page.

iUniverse rev. date: 12/13/2017

PRAISES

"This book presents a revealing account of how the progression of abuse can occur in a marriage and the impact this can have on an entire family. The author shows an open and vulnerable account of her personal experience in hopes that this may be of help to other women in similar situations. It is especially significant to see the road to recovery, out from under the cloud of control, that she was able to take in order to begin to achieve a sense of wholeness and healing. Yet she shows that this is not an easy or quick journey, nor does she minimize her own struggles to have godly responses in this process. Of particular benefit are the helpful and balanced words she shares with those women who also may be victims of controlling men, in hopes that their road to recovery may be aided."

—Dr. Robert D. Larson, Psychologist

I dedicate this book to family and friends who made my recovery possible.

ACKNOWLEDGEMENTS

The Lord gave me four wonderful friends without whom this book may never have made it to fruition. They were eagerly supportive and encouraging. They did editing and offered suggestions. Thank you Ruth Greve, Joy Matlock, Ronda Weaver, and Shirley Wendland.

CONTENTS

ALASKA
present

Old age now applies to me. I have left middle age. I am better off than some and worse off than others. I am neither fat nor thin. If I play the "Wii" just right I can get my age down to 37! In that respect age means nothing. I am plagued with insomnia due to fibromyalgia. My cervical neck presents several complications, any of which could worsen and require surgery. Meanwhile I must take medication every morning and evening to allay the pain. I have not found a doctor who will listen attentively and act appropriately to these maladies. My "cobra" insurance ran out several years ago. There is no affordable insurance for me. Forced to take action just to obtain prescriptions I filled out the reams of paperwork and am now in the state assisted medical system. It is an uncomfortable feeling. I have a new sense of empathy for all those driven into this predicament. We are not all "bottom feeders". Sometimes there is no other choice. This is just one of the many lessons God has taught me thereby making me less judgmental of others.

I am living in Alaska as of 2010. In 2009 I moved my eighty-six year old mother here. My sister and brother-in-law were instrumental in helping me to acquire a couple of part-time jobs. Alaska also has an enormous field of home schooled children which I had hoped would pay off with the grade school spelling series I have authored.

Alaska has actually been a big part of my life for many years; my sister, whom I shall call Rose, was always coming up with new adventures that I should take part in. I owe her a debt of gratitude for including me in positive experiences to prove to myself I was strong in all ways and could accomplish whatever I put my mind to. Her husband also deserves credit in believing in me and encouraging me to tackle seemingly impossible obstacles. I worked for my brother-in-law in his AFLAC office part time and loved it. My sister dropped my name at her company and I have been able to make some big oil bucks teaching CPR/First Aid. This job has allowed me to travel to the

Arctic Ocean; to Kaktovik and Dead Horse (Prudhoe Bay). My sister and husband also put me in charge of organizing their property/business on the west side of Kodiak Island. I worked in the shipyard on a thirty eight foot seiner (fishing vessel) and fed the other six people working there. I took my turn steering the vessel around Kodiak when we hit the open seas with eight foot waves. I have hiked ten miles through swamp land. I have observed Kodiak bears and met a couple of them on a path. I have helped put out a subsistence net and retrieved salmon from it. I am now experienced at wainscoting and running a table saw.

Are you thinking I must be of a fearless and of strong character? You would be wrong. It took many years to build up my self confidence but I want you to see, it is possible.

When I first spent time in Alaska working I stayed with Rose and her husband. Surprise! Marriage is for two people, not three. I returned to Alaska four months later and stayed with my mother in her apartment in Palmer (a town settled by Minnesotans) while seeking out someone through our church in Anchorage to stay with on a part time basis. The daily roundtrip commute of one hundred miles was too much for me and I needed my own space. God did provide a place for me albeit it was short term. This lady had never rented a room before. We agreed on a per month fee based on the fact I would only be there part-time. This worked fine for the job at my brother-in-law's office and teaching CPR/First Aid for Alaska's largest native interest corporation. However, I ended up spending more nights than I expected due to inclement weather. This did not sit well with my landlady. We parted ways. I was discouraged, a state of mind which requires more trust and more prayer. In *God's* time I was led to another lady who has been my salvation. She also went through difficult years of abuse and her husband's involvement in pornography. Since she was able to keep her house she decided she should share the blessing with others. Several Christian women have been helped with a place to stay in her split level home with two bedrooms on the lower level and kitchen privileges upstairs. Since I only stayed part time I paid her per night. When it seemed the right thing for me to live in Alaska I stayed full time with her and trusted the Lord to give me enough money for rent. And of course He has provided. My landlady has become a friend. We take turns cooking, we eat together, we play games, we hike. She leads a recovery group and she has counseled me often as I continue on my path of recovery. The Lord in His wisdom knew I needed more pruning before I was able to write this book.

Meanwhile I gathered some items I needed from thrift stores and from my daughter, Joanne, who began sending me boxes from Minnesota. Oh, there are many more possessions I wish I had with me but once again I have learned how little we need to exist and make a life. Escaping abuse should never be about money worries or leaving possessions behind. God will provide!

I found a church. The sermons are excellent, the singing is great. The people are friendly albeit I have never been visited by anyone or been encouraged to take part in anything. It is hard being a layperson after being a pastor's wife and a pastor's daughter all my life. Luckily I already knew one couple at church from a previous Alaska experience but like my landlady friend the wife is super busy and our time together is minimal.

It is not that easy for me to get out. I have been a home body all of my life, taking care of my younger siblings and the house while my mother worked and then raising my children. I do play bridge a couple times a month (I have one hundred and sixty master points, very important for you to know this) but have not connected to anyone with whom to spend time with outside of bridge. I used to see my mother in Palmer (fifty miles away) every ten days or so but winter, cost of gas, and my insomnia have made that difficult. When I did see her I would stay overnight at my sister's house, but now my nephew and family live there so I have to stay at my mother's assisted living place which is ok but not great. So there are many lonely hours. I do not dwell on meeting a man but I am lonesome for male companionship. It would be nice to know love. I leave this in the Lord's hands. Meanwhile I love where I live. The mountains and seventy foot tall trees make me smile and feel God's awesome creation. And who can't be thrilled at a moose walking down the road or eating off of trees outside your house?

Money is sometimes scarce. Selling my spelling series did not pan out. My brother-in-law lost his position and the Anchorage office so I only put in a few hours at his home office every couple of months. President Obama has squelched further oil drilling so there are fewer employees who need my services teaching CPR/First Aid. I may have to go out into the world and find a job...*Ouch*! I am applying for food stamps, something I never thought I would do. I have started receiving social security checks...Yes! Though it does not amount to much extra, because of my years of marriage I am able to collect off Frederick's social security. This is determined by how many years one was married. A budget is a must. Do not dwell on closed doors but look for open windows. I would not be writing this book if my previously mentioned jobs had stayed active. "I will instruct you and teach you the way you should go; I will counsel you with my eye upon you." (Psalm 32:8)

My children and grandchildren are far away, the reason I did not move to Anchorage sooner. But the Lord provides. My son, Michael, got married and I was able to see the entire clan. This has given me the inner strength to go on. This same son has to fly every few months to Anchorage for business now so that is a great boost. My son, Thomas, also got married. Yeah, another reunion. Skype allows me to see my four grandchildren. I talk with them on the phone once in a while and if I am lucky they are in the mood to sing me a song. I save newspaper photos of all the Alaskan wildlife and send them periodically, although I have been told my children enjoy them as much if not more than my grandchildren. I am expecting two more grandchildren. This makes me very happy!

By some standards I have had a difficult life. However, I see myself as having a full and rewarding life. I desire no new experiences. I do not wish for wealth so that I may enjoy opportunities and material possessions which at present are beyond my reach, although I do have my weak days desiring what I can't afford. My prayer requests are that I may be given more opportunities to serve my God and fellowman and that my children and grandchildren will grow in the understanding of God's love and mature in finding HIS peace. Meanwhile I wait upon the Lord.

Recovery involves forgiveness and moving on. Moving forward means letting go of the past. I am now convinced that this can never fully happen. The sting of abuse recurs frequently. So writing about the history of my abuse dredges up exactly what I am trying to put behind me. I have met many women living under the black cloud of abuse since I aggressively took control of my life. I know there are thousands more existing who have not taken the steps towards recovery or used tough love against their abusers. Forever I did not know where to turn for help, and as most abused women, I kept silent lest the situation reflected on me as a cause to an unsuccessful marriage. Perhaps this book will be read by someone who needs help. I have offered several times to speak to women in the churches to which I have belonged. The pastors were never able to grab hold of the offer and make it happen. It is the nature of the church to keep these abounding predicaments quiet. Friends and family have encouraged me to go ahead with my writing.

Many days I tell the Lord I am ready to go to my eternal home. I can't see that I am being used much in His kingdom. But only the Lord knows the future and what He has planned for us. In these times we meditate, pray, and wait to see what His plans are.

> I will extol thee, my God and King, and bless thy name for ever and ever. Every day I will bless thee, and praise thy name for ever and ever. Great is the Lord, and greatly to be praised, and his greatness is unsearchable…The Lord is faithful in all his words, and gracious in all his deeds. The Lord upholds all who are falling, and raises up all who are bowed down. The eyes of all look to thee, and thou gives them their food in due season. Thou openest thy hand, thou satisfiest the desire of every living thing. The Lord is just in all his ways, and kind in all his doings. The Lord is near to all who call upon him, to all who call upon him in truth. He fulfils the desire of all who fear him, he also hears their cry, and saves them. The Lord preserves all who love him; but all the wicked he will destroy. My mouth will speak the praise of the Lord, and let all flesh bless his holy name for ever and ever.
>
> Psalm 145:1-3, 13-21

WYOMING
shock…..a job to do

Having completed nurse's training in California and having worked long enough to get my feet wet and pay off some bills, I was anxious to leave the "Golden State" of high traffic and materialism. I prayed asking the Lord for direction. I wrote down ten possibilities and placed them in a paper bag. I prayed again, "Thy will be done". I drew the city of my childhood in Wyoming. I gave my two weeks notice, found someone to transport my horse and surviving twin foal, and notified my best friend from nurse's training. Her husband was stationed at the air force base in Cheyenne. I found a job and stayed with my friend until I found an apartment. I easily acquired a job at the hospital in the intensive care unit.

I met Frederick at church. He was the pastor. He was a good speaker, easy to converse with, had a good sense of humor, athletic, musical and not bad looking, and he was available. We were in our late twenties so timing was good. There was an immediate attraction. He came Monday morning after my first visit to church on Sunday. He knocked on the back door. Both of my friends and I worked the three to eleven shift so sleeping in the morning and being downstairs we did not hear the knock. Tuesday he came again…a little later. This time he came downstairs and knocked. We still did not hear his knock. Wednesday he came yet again… a little later. We were not only up but outside leaving to do laundry when he was emerging from his car. We talked and my friend Londa ended up inviting him over for dinner which she informed him I would be cooking. A couple of weeks later my friends asked to take religious instructions from him which would take place in our apartment. After one such lesson Frederick asked if we knew anyone who would help him type up an instruction course he had inherited from his seminary vicar year. Londa all but pushed me out the door. Typing led to a meal and a romp on the floor and kissing. There was not much to dating because he didn't like to spend money. My friends talked him into some outings but soon they left for Germany and our lives centered mostly around church work and just stopping in to see each other. There were red lights. There were study clubs involving not just area pastors but also their families which he never took me to.

Once I asked Frederick if my friends and I could attend a traveling seminary concert with him a hundred miles away. I love music and I was excited for my friends to have this spiritual experience. After the concert the "called workers" (pastors and teachers) had a get-together at the parsonage. Immediately upon entering the house Frederick separated himself from us. We found an unoccupied couch and sat down. No one talked to us. Everyone except us was offered an alcoholic drink…we were offered a soft drink. I followed this up with a visit to the kitchen and asked for a shot of whiskey in my soft drink. Boy oh boy did I get a look! This was reported to Frederick with a twist; I had *grabbed* the bottle and poured it myself.

Another time when my sister was visiting we begged a ride from Frederick to Denver where he had a get-together. We were dropped off at the zoo as we requested. As the afternoon wore on and no Frederick we called and asked him to pick us up. Upon arriving back at his host's place, he left us at the car and went back inside. We sat on the curb…no one invited us in. Finally we boldly "crashed the party". We were treated as outsiders with leprosy.

Our physical contact was beyond acceptable dating interaction. I was convinced he was just shy about proposing or he would not be so physically aggressive. Once in what I figured was a desperate try to sever himself from his attraction to me, a most unlikely conservative pastor's wife, he made a date with a teacher. It was the only date but I was shocked. I questioned him on the integrity of being so deeply involved with me and without any discussion deciding to "play the field". The discussion was just that short.

My presence was also not requested when his parents came to visit. I was from California after all and my clothes said so from patched jeans to short dresses and long straight sun bleached hair. There was almost no talk of a future. It appeared there was a rule that dating must take place for two years before entering a permanent relationship. Every so often I ended our relationship only to come back when he again pursued me. Finally I decided to move away and end it (good decision). He found out my plan and in the most miserable attempt ever known to the world of romance indicated an engagement was in order. I arrived at work late wondering if he actually had asked me to marry him. My co-workers sent me away (we were not busy) to confirm his intent and not return until I had; they were sick of hearing about our relationship. Frederick was at a meeting so I visited some friends, my grade school teacher and his wife. They too were sick of hearing the ups and downs of our relationship. They invited Frederick over after his meeting and asked if we were engaged to which he responded, "I guess so" and they poured drinks (Frederick very seldom drank) and insisted on celebrating which was very big of them as the lady always warned me this wasn't going to work. Some days later we talked about setting a date and he brought up looking for rings. At the time I did not have any interest in a diamond. Boy he liked that! Some weeks later I was at his place. He seemed more somber than usual and distant. He was downstairs in his study, said he was checking in his theological books to see how binding engagement really was. He did not laugh. I went in the bathroom and cried. Of course, he was just scared I told myself. Everything would be fine after we were married, right?

The year after I moved to Wyoming my brother and his wife followed. They lived thirty miles from us. Now at least there was family to spend some time with. My sister-in-law started taking religious instructions from Frederick. I used my brother on many occasions as a sounding board. One time in particular comes to mind before we were engaged. I was on a particularly traumatic emotional roller coaster ride trying to understand Frederick's behavior. I lay in bed crying. Glancing up into the kitchen I spied my knives hanging on the wall. In despair I had a weak moment when I actually considered using one. Quickly I ran to the phone and called my brother. Thirty minutes later he was in my apartment. Even now as I write this I cannot believe I descended to that level of thinking. My father explained once that I was the "forbidden fruit". Even though Frederick was attracted to me I did not fit the picture of a typical Midwestern pastor's wife.

A date was set. My sister-in-law was excited about helping plan the wedding reception. Alas, it was not to be. I was at work one evening when there was a knock on the intensive care door where I worked. It was Frederick. He had just received a call from my brother asking Frederick to come immediately. The only thing my brother could tell Frederick was that his wife was in the hospital on a respirator. I was able to leave work and go with him. My sister-in-law had suffered a cerebral aneurysm and was brain dead. I called her parents and then mine. Her parents were of course in a state of shock so my parents arranged travel from California and facilitated their immediate departure. Only when my father arrived did we finally pray together. The doctor then suggested a "no resuscitation" order; her heart stopped the next day just after my brother went home for the first time. One further note; only one month earlier she had become insistent on being baptized, almost panicky that it had to be done now. Frederick baptized her. This now was his first funeral. It was extremely difficult but he handled it well.

Briefly we talked of postponing the wedding but did not. My matron of honor flew from Germany as she had promised, since she encouraged the relationship from the beginning. I had a small apartment so get-togethers centered at the church parsonage, Frederick's home. Frederick refused a bachelor outing so he and his best man left for the evening leaving both sets of parents, the best man's wife, my matron of honor, a member of the church who had come for the bachelor party, and me. My father made the drinks. Coming back down the hall from the bathroom my father joked, "Daughter, you could have waited to move your clothes into the bedroom until after the wedding." Of course I hadn't and we (not his mother) laughed at his joke. My father asked if anyone wanted drink refills. Frederick's mother vehemently declined. The next day as I am with my sisters and matron of honor getting ready, Frederick comes to my door. His mother did not sleep due to the drinking and "off-colored" jokes. It definitely would have been a good move to call off the wedding, and in my defense, I did think of it.

My father, a minister, was not allowed to perform the ceremony as he was of a different church body. He never got over this hurt. When we left for the reception, Frederick told his parents they could follow us. Bless his best man, who stopped the car when he found this out, went back and gave his parents directions to the reception, and then drove us around town encouraging Frederick to embrace me. Frederick's parents, of course, were not speaking to my parents at the reception or to anyone else for that matter. There was drinking! One pastor spoke before toasting and suggested that if Frederick treated me as well as his BMW, our marriage would be successful. Ah, another fleeting moment of clarity. I knew that would never happen. Life began as with most newlyweds. We had a two day honeymoon (it was supposed to be only one but he was tired) even though his father had offered to preach on Sunday.

The next week Frederick was off to a three day conference. I was anxious to be the perfect wife to a fault. I cleaned out closets, reorganized, and put wedding presents away. When he returned home I fixed three meals a day and not from cans or packages. Frederick was thrilled when I was too tired (pregnant) to fix breakfast and he could finally get back to his cereal routine. We did nothing together…no walks, no games, no movies, no outings. He did his work, took his afternoon nap and in the evening watched TV. I worked two or three times a week at the hospital. As when dating, he loved this part of me. He listened intently to the stories I would bring back about hospital drama. I think I should never have completely quit.

Decorating one's home can be a source of gratification for a housewife. Just before Frederick and I were engaged, the church parsonage was finished. Frederick and his mother went shopping. They purchased everything to furnish the house, a complete bedroom set, a used dining room table and chairs and an ugly used sofa. Frederick already had an old chair for the living room. After our marriage I felt like I was living in his mother's house. Even an old picture had to be hung because his mother gave it to him. Little by little I was able to make it more our home in spite of Frederick's resistance. Finally, with his approval I was able to purchase a new couch. The old couch went to the basement, *hurrah*! I did try to leave the bedroom set when we moved but lost on that one. Twenty-seven years later when I finally left, in one of his few positive emails to me, he offered to purchase a new bedroom set if I would return home.

Our actual honeymoon took place in June. I had no prior knowledge of this. Frederick had worked his summers during seminary at Glacier Park, Montana. He wanted to revisit his old stomping grounds. This was our first long distance trip together; a prelude of many trips to come. We stopped when he wanted to stop, which wasn't very often. I am not a great car traveler but had to endure. Frederick had shown me pictures while we were dating and now related again the beauty and grandeur of the park including the magnificent hotels. I was looking forward to experiencing what he had planted in my mind. Well, we passed the beautiful hotels and ended up in a circle of rustic, white, one-bedroom cottages with a communal bathroom in the center. Hmmmm, not what I understood would be our accommodations. I knew he didn't part with money easily but this put a new slant on things. The first day was spent in revisiting places from his memory including the red tour buses which he had driven. I was anxious to hike in the truly beautiful surroundings but tried to be patient. We went inside one of the hotels and he wandered around looking for anyone he still might know. This was another week into my most likely pregnancy, the time when you need to not let your stomach get completely empty. My desire to eat fell on deaf ears. Finally he met a kindred spirit to converse with. A half an hour into their conversation I said I needed to eat and would meet him at an eatery I spied across the grounds. Alas, I was not carrying any cash and had to return, now feeling very nauseous. Luckily he was finished visiting and also feeling hungry. We then went for the long anticipated hike. He warned me of the grizzlies and the attacks that were occasionally made in Glacier Park. In spite of this, on the return, he walked so far ahead of me he was lost to sight. I had water but we had not purchased snacks and I was becoming weak and tired. I began hearing every twig snap. I decided my best chance, should I see a bear, was to go downhill to the lake. No bears, made it back safely.

One of the features at the hotels was an evening sing-a-long. Frederick took me to the bar first and bought me a drink. I'm not sure this ever happened again until we had counseling in Milwaukee twenty-seven years later. At the sing-a-long everyone sat on the floor. I found a spot. Instead of sitting next to me Frederick sat a few rows behind. I remember these seemingly little incidences because I was still a newlywed and each of these hurt deeply. Reluctantly, the next day Frederick rented a canoe. I had rowed before but only a few times. He became very impatient with my beginner's knowledge of rowing, to the point he was curt and cutting. When we reached the other side of the lake I hopped out and said I would walk back. That night in bed I turned away from him hurt and mortified at what the future of my marriage looked like. It wasn't long before I jumped over him and made it to the kitchen sink in time to throw up. He actually got up and showed some empathy, something that would not happen often in the next twenty-six years. And there was somewhat of an apology for the canoe trip.

I, Anya, began to write New Year's letters to family and friends. You will see that I portray a loving family scenario. Of course I would not tell the sad truths of our marriage.

Newsletter – 1976

After two days of fighting to stay in my warm, cozy, private environment, the doctor, nurses, father, and mother took sides against me and forced me out into the cold, cruel world. My mother didn't seem to enjoy the affair too much but my father, who was right there all the time putting all his Lamaze knowledge into practice, sounded excited, said I was ugly, and then deftly cut me away from my mother. The doctor correctly guessed that I was 6# 2oz. I'm only 18 inches long, but I make up for that with my big feet. I also have lots more hair than my daddy. My maternal Grandma says I have a sassy little mouth like my mother.

I was so good in the hospital that mother decided to come home after a day and a half. I sure didn't make it easy for her the first few days at home. Recently, however, I have heard them say that my disposition and general behavior is improving considerably. Actually, I think that they've just learned to take care of me a little better.

Thomas

Frederick was happy with the pregnancy as long as it didn't interfere with his needs. So if I said at lunch time I didn't feel well, he replied, "What's for lunch?" And I would drag myself to the kitchen and accommodate him. On a trip to see his parents I told him I was feeling sick and needed to stop for something light to eat, a salad or a bowl of soup. He stopped at a rest stop and ate the chicken he had packed. Just the thought of cold fried chicken was enough to cause me pangs of nausea. As we made our way through Chicago traffic I again said I needed to stop. He became angry that I was not helping him maneuver through traffic.

My car was sold after I quit work, so with a baby I started my years of being housebound. The mission congregation was small but Frederick now stayed away more evenings than before. One lonely evening I called some close friends of my parents, now close friends of mine, only to find out Frederick was there visiting them at 9:00 p.m. I confronted him the next day asking why he would stop there instead of coming home. I explained I was lonely and it would be nice to spend some time with him in the evening. He became defensive about his need to stay in contact with the church president.

Of course, I knew Frederick stopped many times during the day at the president's work place. I also knew when he stopped at their home, food and drink were brought out. Our discussion escalated to yelling at which point I declared him selfish for not putting my needs first. *Wrong thing to say!* He exploded and raised his arm to swing. Not wanting my son to witness whatever was about to happen, I edged my way into the hall where I was slapped multiple times, (my glasses went flying) as he informed me I should never call him selfish again (and I never did). As soon as possible I escaped to the bedroom. I flopped on the bed, devastated and crying. He followed, turned me on my back and with some restraint, slapped at me a couple more times, at the same time saying he was sorry but I provoked him.

> I cry with my voice to the Lord, with my voice I make supplication to the Lord, I pour out my complaint before him, I tell my trouble before him. When my spirit is faint, thou knowest my way!
>
> Psalm 142:1-3

Two life patterns immerged somewhere in this time frame. We were now codependents in an abusive relationship. Frederick saw my inadequacies as reason for his abusive behavior. I saw his abusive behavior as reason for my self-pity and resentment. Our marriage was as far away from Christ centered as you can get. The other pattern was my determination to maintain some semblance of self-worth. I was determined not to let his belittling make me feel I was a lesser person than others.

Newsletter – 1977

August brought Anya's parents to Wyoming. We spent three glorious days with them and Anya's brother in the mountains though Anya was not always feeling up to par especially in the mornings?!?!?

In October we made it to Anya's parents in Indio, California via Salt Lake City for a conference. What about Anya's solo trip through Salt Lake City???...don't ask!! In November we first found out that our expected baby would be two babies.

Frederick's mother came out for three weeks in January to help out while Anya got her rest. And for two months we made weekly visits to a DR. in Colorado, to make sure all was going well. At home we began setting up for twins. Anya's mother arrived the end of February to help with the babies who didn't come and didn't come as the doctor predicted. After one month of intermittent labor they finally arrived, weighing in at 5# 10 oz. and 6# 1 oz. Michael had an immediate transfusion for low blood count and by the next morning was doing fine.

Our lives have changed slightly. We take turns eating, sleeping, and running errands. Thomas bangs his head against the doors and walls to relieve his frustrations. We had three days interim between Anya's mother's departure and Frederick's mother's second arrival. It was scary, but we managed to survive.

We enjoyed all of our company last summer even though sometimes we were caught changing the sheets as you walked in the door.

The year ended on a sad but happy note. Frederick's father died suddenly. Frederick flew home and spent a week with his mother.

Yes, I was pregnant again. I grew by leaps and bounds. I just figured I had not had time to regain my abdominal integrity. On a visit to my elderly family doctor for Thomas's checkup the doctor gave me a hard time for being pregnant again…in a friendly way. I looked two months further along than what I was. He felt my belly and proclaimed I was having twins, to which I replied, *"No Way!"* On my first visit to my obstetrician I begged him to tell me it wasn't so. He said it was too early to tell. He would do an ultrasound when I returned from vacation. All I could wear from three months on was maternity clothes. After the ultrasound, during which I cranked my head to watch and was convinced there was only one baby, Frederick and I sat in the waiting room until the rest of the patients were gone. Only then did the doctor call us back to his office. His declaration left me shocked. I guess I just couldn't imagine two more babies at this time. We were then ushered to their little kitchen for cheese and crackers…a little celebration. I did receive some help with cleaning when my obstetrician ordered me at six months to refrain from using stairs and doing any heavy housework. Of course, I still made three meals a day and totally took care of Thomas.

The night I was supposed to be picked up from the hospital after the twins were born, was a church night during Lent. Church would have been out at 7:45 p.m. so with haste and much consideration Frederick could have been to the hospital by 9:00 p.m. But he was so busy acting the proud father he arrived at 10:30 p.m. I had been sitting in the lobby for over an hour as they needed my bed. Michael and Paul were crying as it was time again for them to eat. In his haste to make up for his late departure he forgot the nicely packed suitcase with the twins' clothes. So, they had to be carted home in their hospital gowns and wrapped for the yet cold weather in two dirty blankets kept in the car. Thankfully my mother was still up to comfort and care for me.

I half nursed and half bottle fed the twins therefore Frederick could have offered to take a night feeding but he didn't. Frederick controlled the temperature of the house. It did not matter how cold I was getting up in the middle of the night. I was so sleep deprived I slept fast and hard, so much so, that when the babies beckoned, I awoke with sweat soaked pajamas which had to be changed before answering their frenzied cries. Before he went to his study in the morning he turned the temperature up but kept our bathroom door closed so the bathroom would be toasty warm for his shower. My mother sat with me one morning during a feeding and questioned why the heat couldn't be turned up. After hearing the reason she immediately opened the bathroom door. What could Frederick say to his mother-in-law? Things went back to *normal* after she left. Finally, because I was up and down all night disturbing Frederick's sleep, he purchased a twin bedroom set so I could be moved into the twin's bedroom. I was given a space heater so at least I was warm.

> Cast your burden on the Lord, and he will sustain you; he will never permit the righteous to be moved.
>
> Psalm 55:22

The day my mother left, both the twins and I had doctor's visits. Frederick took the twins and Thomas. When I arrived after my appointment there were two doctors talking to Frederick and two diapered but naked babies on the exam table screaming their heads off – Men! After I entered the room Thomas resumed his place at the door banging his head. One of the doctors looked at me and asked how everything was going. I broke down crying.

He gave me some very sage advice. "If anyone offers to help you, say yes!" I needed to hear this as I was very independent.

Once and awhile we loaded up the children and did grocery shopping together. Of course we were frequently stopped in the store by people in awe of the twins. I would continue shopping by myself as Frederick played the proud father.

Newsletter – 1978

Thank-you Frederick's mother for keeping up the house in January so Anya could follow the Doctor's orders and get plenty of rest. Thank-you for all your help in March and April after the twins arrived and once again in October when your canning and freezing were especially appreciated.

Thank-you Anya's mother for your patience as we waited two weeks past the Doctor's due date for the twins to arrive, and most of all for the following week spoiling us all and getting us off on the right foot. Thank-you Anya's father for lending her out and *roughing* it.

Thank-you nurses for the eighteen boxes of pampers, hot dishes, and other delicious goodies. Thank-you for coming to the rescue along with the ladies in the congregation when Anya had her hypoglycemic attack following minor surgery on her wrist. Thank-you sister for the week spent in July cooking, cleaning, washing, consoling and playing with your darling nephews.

Thank-you brother and sister-in-law for doing so much during the past year keeping our house in order, babysitting, and providing some relaxation by playing Bridge with us. Thank-you dear nanny who upon returning from school in June was immediately hired for two hours a day, six days a week, to put our house in order and give us time to take it a little easier.

Thank-you LORD for seeing us through 1978 and especially for the gift of your son whose birthday we have once again celebrated with song, worship, and sharing of gifts. May we all thank Him through 1979 for the many undeserved blessings we are sure to receive.

Thomas would have benefited the most from time with his father. He so needed to escape the "nursery" but I just could not talk Frederick into this. Thomas regressed physically but continued to spiral mentally. He played well if he had something challenging. I found a puzzle for three year olds which kept him occupied until he was fifteen months old. So I found a puzzle game for five year olds. He was a great help to me. He could fetch anything I asked him to get. He helped feed, holding the bottle patiently. I found a third infant seat to make Thomas feel like part of the group. He would stack a pile of twelve books next to his seat and read to Paul and Michael for an hour. This was an enormous blessing as Paul and Michael were very difficult babies. They cried a lot and took mini-naps. My family doctor gave me some Phenobarbital for them at our first well baby visit. This was great...instead of sleeping only fifteen minutes, they now slept thirty minutes.

Over many years I had developed a weakness in my right wrist. With a certain movement it would become sore. An ace bandage or a wrist support worn for twenty-four hours would eliminate the pain. But gradually it took two days and longer. Shortly after the twins were born it resurfaced. Only this time it just would not go away. I sought medical help which resulted in outpatient surgery (it was an extra tendon). I was told this was trivial and I could immediately resume normal activities (I don't think his activities included taking care of three babies and a husband). On the way home from the hospital (a mere two miles) the anesthetic already wore off. The pain was so severe I was in tears upon arriving home and immediately sent Frederick to the pharmacy for pain medication. Ladies from the church, upon hearing of my predicament, offered their help in shifts. The next day the noon relief did not show up. I had just finished feeding the twins with help from Thomas. Luckily my brother and his wife showed up on their lunch breaks and put the children down for their naps. I had taken a pain pill after breakfast. It was now 1:00 pm and I had not eaten. I was so tired and weak from hunger I stayed on the living room floor and fell asleep. The last sound I remembered was Paul crying. The door slammed as Frederick returned home from a visitation and I awakened. I exclaimed that Paul was crying (he really wasn't anymore). I knew I had to eat! While Frederick was in the bathroom, I forced myself to rise, went into the kitchen, grabbed something out of the refrigerator and put it on the stove to heat. Frederick came in, sat down with his McDonald's bag, and began eating. In a few seconds I lost consciousness and slithered down to the floor. No comment from Frederick. In a couple of minutes he remarked about the food heating up and when he got no response from me, he got up, stepped over my head, turned the stove off, stepped back over me, and resumed his lunch. I was trying to will myself to speak or move an arm but just couldn't make it happen. All I had was my hearing. I heard the paper rattling; I heard Frederick eating. After he finished he came over, called my name and shook me a little. Then he was on the phone with a nurse friend who lived a short distance from us. He informed her lightheartedly that I had decided to take a nap on the kitchen floor. There was no urgency in his voice. Then there was silence until the nurse showed up at the door. She checked my vital signs which were fine and said there was nothing to do but take me to the emergency room. If only I could have let them know to give me some sugar. Being carried as dead weight is at the top of my list for worst things to experience, (well, second to being slapped). I slept on the way to the hospital. I awoke on the guerney in the emergency room. I heard the doctor talking to Frederick. My blood sugar level was low normal. Upon discussing my wrist surgery and pain medication the doctor asked how many pills I might have taken. Ouch… Frederick did not insist there was no way I would overdose. He just left that idea hang out there. Meanwhile the aide came to check my vital signs. There was an IV in my left hand which is why I am sure she chose to take my blood pressure on my right arm, a decision I'm sure she still regrets. She grabbed my bandaged wrist to lift my arm in order to put on the blood pressure cuff. The pain was immediate and excruciating!! I sat up, let out a blood curdling scream, and dropped back down unconscious. I wonder how many times she has related this experience. Soon the IV infusion of dextrose elevated my blood sugar enough that I regained consciousness. I finally could say, "I'm hungry!" I was given a sandwich and juice. Frederick came over, smiled, and remarked that I looked better, then excused himself to visit a patient as long as we were at the hospital. I immediately put my knowledge of how little Frederick cared for me as far back in my subconscious as it would go. "Hear my cry, O God, listen to my prayer; from the end of the earth I call to thee, when my heart is faint. Lead thou me to the rock that is higher than I; for thou art my refuge, a strong tower against the enemy." (Psalm 61:1-3) It was seventeen years before I let it surface and related the incidence to a counselor, a counselor who believed me unlike her peer who assured Frederick that a semiconscious person would not be able to give details in a time ordered manner. I doubt he was an authority on this subject.

A couple of months later I uttered a plea that we have some time together. The discussion escalated ending in another angry tirade. I again made it to the hallway out of the viewing range of our three children, anticipating slapping would be my punishment for challenging his priorities. As he raised his arm to deliver the blows I remembered what my father had told me. I exclaimed, "If you slap me I will go to the elders." It did not have the affect my father thought it would. He slapped me back and forth longer than the first time. This time I went all the way to our bathroom and locked the door. Oh, there were sorrys again complete with… if I didn't make him so upset…if I this…and if I that. His temper was clearly justified and the onset thereof most definitely my fault.

> Be merciful to me, O God, be merciful to me, for in thee my soul takes refuge; in the shadow of thy wings I will take refuge, till the storms of destruction pass by. I cry to God Most High, to God who fulfils his purpose for me. He will send from heaven and save me, he will put to shame those who trample upon me. God will send forth his steadfast love and his faithfulness!
>
> Psalm 57:1-3

My mother-in-law visited every year. I never quite figured out Frederick's relationship with his mother, but I was like a ghost during her visits. They talked without me, she helped him with paperwork and he brought her anything from his closet that needed mending. She literally jumped to serve him. They ate breakfast together totally ignoring Thomas while I was busy taking care of the twins. One morning as I went about my daily care-giving, they talked and then they were gone. Out the door without a word! I was hurt! I truly felt like I didn't exist. When I had a chance I went down to Frederick's study and wrote him how I felt. I'm sure I mentioned something about a husband-wife relationship. Soon after he arrived home (without a word to me) he went to his study. He came upstairs with nostrils flaring. I was escorted to a back bedroom and the door was closed. What an ungrateful wretch I was! I showed no appreciation for all the help his mother extended. There were just not enough words to describe my selfishness. Another rule was made. I was never to write him a letter again! He left. I cried. Life continued. At this point I think I just crawled into myself and was very careful never to let a discussion get heated. I was careful not to say anything confrontational. And I was pregnant again. I was just keeping my head above water.

> Fear not, for I have redeemed you; I have called you by name, you are mine. When you pass through the waters I will be with you; and through the rivers, they shall not overwhelm you; when you walk through fire you shall not be burned, and the flame shall not consume you. For I am the Lord your God, the Holy One of Israel your Savior.
>
> Isaiah 43:1-3

Newsletter – 1979

APRIL– After celebrating three birthdays in March, sister Susan arrives on the 10th to help ready things for the expected baby in May. Anya goes into labor on the 11th (Holy Week) and gives Susan and sister-in-law a crash course on how to take care of three boys and live to tell about it. On Maundy Thursday we proceed on the yearly trek to Colorado for delivery. That afternoon there are groanings which cannot be uttered as Anya labors over the baby and Frederick labors over his sermon for that evening. Labor is successful in both cases and we have Marie weighing in prematurely at 5# 151/2 oz. She is much weightier than the sermon, but the sermon is longer, 20 compared to eighteen.

MAY– Michael and Paul each get their first tooth, three days apart, at thirteen and a half months.

JUNE– Summer comes and everybody is outside – Yeah!! Life improves by 65%. Our faithful nanny is back from school and helps us with cleaning, laundry, and babysitting.

JULY– Nanny gets a full time job – bye, bye. We find a replacement to help. Marie gets her bangs cut. Thomas hits his forehead on the edge of his bed and goes to the emergency room for three stitches.

AUGUST– We lose our morning help. Our long awaited vacation in southwestern Colorado with Anya's parents is cancelled due to the news that her father has cancer. After a week of phone calls from Anya's mother, it is obvious that she could use some emotional support so we decide to vacation for a week in California. Our airplane flight over was well planned, but the airlines blew it. We drove to Denver to find that our plane was late, so then we would miss our connection in Phoenix. Instead we fly to San Diego, then to Los Angeles, and finally to Palm Springs, arriving six hours late, having missed three planes, in vain running down concourses, having spent three hours in San Diego without a chance to call sister Susan, and the last three hours of our ordeal having three boys without any diapers!!! Anyway, Anya's father came through surgery fine, improved rapidly, and we had a nice three day visit with him after he came home.

SEPTEMBER– Thomas opens an *unopenable* bottle of Tylenol for a snack. The first challenge is to get him to throw up, the second, to get him to stop. Once again we can peaches, pears, and applesauce. Michael can now say, "No pray" in exerting his Christian liberty.

OCTOBER– Anya is losing weight and wearing her winter clothes for the first time in four years. Frederick's mother visits for two weeks. Paul hits his head on the same bed as Thomas and gets six stitches. Marie has two teeth. Michael insists that the boy in the mirror is Paul!

NOVEMBER– No colds…flu instead! Fifteen dirty diapers a day. Thomas informs us, "Mine be stinkpot." Thomas can tell the twins apart but won't tell Daddy his secret. Paul hits corner of the end table and gets four stitches in his lip.

DECEMBER– Frederick and Anya are invited to a nearby Dinner Playhouse for dinner and "Camelot". We have a nice Christmas with Anya's brother and wife.

JANUARY– The flu bug visits with us again and Anya is pregnant - don't know what bug that is. Thomas pins himself between his bed and the wall with a cardboard box and has to be extricated. Haven't figured that one out.

FEBRUARY– Anya is sick and everyone suffers. Marie is our earliest walker at ten months.

MARCH– Birthdays again!

APRIL– Marie is one year old. Frederick declines the call to a large congregation in Milwaukee. We enjoy some beautiful weather after a record winter snowfall of 117 inches.

We wish you all the Lord's blessings.

My sister had no experience with children. She also had to be shown where baby items were as I had not yet organized for the new baby. The doctor thought it was a false alarm but decided to keep me overnight as we lived an hour away. Several hours later (no surprise to me) I had a baby girl and Frederick hurried off for church. My little girl was the easiest of the babies except her late night fussy time. I would get to bed at midnight or one, get up during the night for a feeding and still my day started at 6:00 a.m. No help from Frederick.

A word about that horrible trip to California. In San Diego Frederick decided to talk to the airlines about the $20 extra we had to pay when our flight was changed due to their error. I waited with the four children, ate lunch, observed the plane land, load, and take off. After a half an hour, I decided to go down the corridor Frederick had taken. I had to carry the baby and paraphernalia so the three boys, ages two and one, had to walk. A lady in a big hurry ran into one of the twins with her suitcase. He was unhurt and she apologized but I still have an occasional nightmare. I spied Frederick almost to the front of the line. We missed our flight to save $20 which customer service was unable to help with. My father, with great diplomacy, chided him for his thoughtlessness to his family.

Newsletter - 1980

Joanne arrived on time, the largest baby of them all and the easiest baby by far.

Marie walked at ten months, ran at eleven months and climbed at twelve months. She plays second mother to everyone, plays second fiddle to no one!

Michael was kind enough to keep his strep throat to himself. Now states, "Jesus likes me to hit Marie."

Paul has a good tenor voice and likes to dance. Hovers over Joanne. Likes to help clear the table.

Thomas started Sunday School in October. Checks the heavens to see if he can find Jesus. Manages the household!

Anya has time to waste with only two in diapers. Only fifteen loads of laundry/week.

Frederick specializes in washing diapers and dishes and giving horse rides. He also preaches on Sunday!

We visited Frederick's relatives the end of May.

Anya's parents spent a few days in July.

Not much gardening but did do our usual canning.

Greetings in the name of our risen Lord.

Whoops, didn't use that diaphragm one night and I was pregnant again. I was perpetually tired just doing the basics; feeding and dressing. And then there was another girl. I never bounced back from this pregnancy. "My flesh and my heart may fail, but God is the strength of my heart and my portion forever." (Psalm 73:26)

A typical day now was up at 7:00 a.m., change five diapers, put the middle three children in their high chairs and the baby in her recliner seat. Thomas took his position at the counter chair to make toast. At three years old he made toast every morning. Frederick did help with breakfast at this point making the main course of hot cereal or eggs etc. I poured juice and started serving. Frederick asked me one morning while I was nursing baby five at 10:00 a.m., why I was so grumpy. I told him I had no time for *my* breakfast. Typical display of martyrdom. For the next couple of months Frederick came up from the study and made me breakfast…Wow! After the baby was fed and put down for a morning nap, there was cleanup, another round of diaper changes, and dressing the other four, who were then put in their rooms for play time while I showered and dressed. Soon it was time for lunch which I handled alone. Then everyone including Frederick went down for a nap. This gave me time for laundry and supper planning. After nap time another round of diapers and a planned activity such as coloring or playing a record. And then supper time. Once in a while Frederick showed up and played with the children while I made supper. After some play time there were baths and reading books before bed at 7:00 p.m. Now I could do dishes if Frederick had not done them and clean up the house so I was ready for another day. I also had a full day of dirty diapers to rinse out...I just did not have time during the day to take care of this. This must have seemed pitiful even to Frederick who grabbed the diaper pail every morning on his way down to the study, and threw them in the wash. Dry, clean diapers appeared mid-morning.

At some point I decided devotions should be started with the children. I presented this to Frederick. No answer. I did them alone. One evening we were just ready to begin when Frederick walked through. I asked him to take over. He mumbled something, shook his head, and went downstairs to his office. Mind boggling. How could a pastor not be interested in devotions with his children?

Thank God for the telephone, permitting me to reach out and touch someone. Sometimes during the week this was my only link to the outside. I usually made it to bed by midnight. Frederick turned in at 10:00 p.m.

One Sunday I was sick along with all five children. After church Frederick had lunch and then left to help some members pack for moving. Oh, there were others to help but it was part of his "pastoral obligations". Most Sundays I made it to church with no help, but if there was any upset in the routine I just gave up. Once in a while some members helped. These same adopted parents/grandparents sat with me in church. I still on occasion played the organ sometimes with as little as two hours notice. I am not an accomplished musician…I need practice! Frederick expected me to do this.

I never quit bleeding after delivering Joanne. Finally, the doctor suggested a D&C just to make sure all the placenta had been removed. Well, as long as I was going in I decided to have two wisdom teeth pulled (I had two pulled ten years earlier under a local and there was much pain). This double procedure threw the hospital into a frenzy. I received many calls questioning my intent and the feasibility of this proposed madness. I suggested one doctor would not know what the other was doing, working on opposite ends. I remember no pain from the D&C….wish I could say the same for my mouth. Another dry socket! After the first extraction ten years earlier, the dentist said the dry socket occurred because I was too active… this time I was told it was because I was not active enough.

Newsletter - 1981

Excuses for another late New Year's letter:
- December pregnancy followed by an early miscarriage
- Two week vacation in California this February
- Frederick's call to Texas

Family - The Year of Teeth:
- Frederick had eight cavities
- Anya had two wisdom teeth removed
- Paul and Michael at three and ½ finally get their two year molars
- Joanne gets her first tooth at fourteen months, three days

Vacation Week in the mountains in sunny July:
- used a 22' trailer from some friends
- originally planned for nine days
- last minute funeral reduces it to seven days
- emergency illness and Frederick returns to congregation for the weekend
- Frederick returns Sunday with mother and stepfather
- left two days early due to critically ill church member, reducing vacation to five days
- funeral three days later
- did have wonderful time with four families from congregation

However, Frederick did not feel this counted as a vacation
so we decided to visit in
- California and miss two weeks of winter.
- our nanny came with…yeah!
- Las Vegas: brother and family
- Anya was a good steward of the quarter generously given by husband. Made $2.50 on the second nickel.
- brother takes us to Caesar's Palace to see Frank Sinatra
- Indio: Anya's parents, brother and surprise….sister and family
- fresh squeezed grapefruit for breakfast
- Anya loses voice (no comments necessary)
- Jacuzzi at brother's house enjoyed by eight children
- San Diego: Sister and husband
- Harbor Cruise was delightful
- enjoyed beach though it was cold

- San Fernando Valley: Cousin and family
- meals and bridge on patio after children were in bed
- everyone comes down with colds!
- relaxing day at Griffeth Park Zoo

Garden produces bumper crop!

- eating, canning, freezing, and sharing
- plus bought and canned peaches, pears, tomatoes, applesauce, and sauerkraut

Odds N Ends

- Thomas says his Sunday School teacher wrote the Bible
- Michael and Paul discussed transplanting the hair on Daddy's chest to his head
- Marie gives detailed instructions to her brothers on how to care for her baby (doll) while she is out
- Joanne's siblings; "she don't know nothing yet"

P.S. Anya's father responding well to chemotherapy

P.S.P.S. We are moving to Texas!!

I never forgot my diaphragm now! I made a doctor's appointment when monthly bleeding did not quit. He said I was on the brink of a miscarriage. I insisted I had to go to the store first and get disposable diapers and some easy supper for Frederick. Having accomplished this I returned to the doctor for a D&C. He explained there was a lot of tissue but nothing formed. My hormones were worn out. After an hour I was high on the Demerol. My brother and sister-in-law found out I was at the doctor's office alone and came over. I'm sure my sister-in-law gave Frederick a piece of her mind for he found a babysitter and showed up almost the same time. The next morning, having hit the down side of the Demerol and emotional upset from the procedure, I lay on the couch after breakfast, still in my bathrobe. The children loved it. They played all over me. My sister-in-law called to ask how I was. I cried. She told me to hang up and not answer the phone. She called and Frederick answered downstairs. In a minute he was upstairs offering to help. He said he would have helped more but he had January paperwork to complete for the church.

We did have an agreement that our vacations would be on a three year cycle. One year to his relatives, one year to mine, and one year our own family vacation. This would be the year for ourselves. It took a reminder of our agreement to make it happen. In the loaned camper we were able to squish the four children together on one side which left the other pullout for Frederick and me. The youngest, Joanne, for her own protection, slept in the cupboard above the beds. The Lord knew I would never have been able to manage this on my own. He provided many arms for holding and keeping track of the children. We established our ritual at bedtime. One at a time I did a quick wipe down of the day's dirt. Each time I went outside for another one I was given my swallow of wine. Oh, did I mention Frederick also invited his mother and step-father? This meant he had to leave us for an entire day to meet them. As long as he was doing this he might as well make a hospital visit. He left again the next evening to make a phone call and check on the hospitalized member. The man had died. So our vacation was cut short which was actually fine because the second night the baby awoke in the middle of the night crying. Bringing her into bed with me it was obvious she was running a high fever. Her fever broke the next day but she was still fussy and miserable. By the time we arrived home she had a rash...the measles!

One morning I felt worse than usual. Feeling like I couldn't take it another minute my mind began planning an escape. I thought about the car but decided Frederick would see or hear me from his study on the lower level and be able to stop me before I got out of the driveway. In a crazy moment I pulled the couch in front of the stairs so my six month old wouldn't fall down and with no shoes walked out the door and just kept walking, never turning back. I walked over a mile to a friend's house. On the way I passed the young girl on a bicycle who came over a couple mornings a week to help out. I told her not to lie, but if not asked, she did not need to say anything to Frederick. My friend asked if I needed something to eat. I said no but could I lie down on a bed? I slept three hours! Meanwhile Frederick, having obtained information from the babysitter, had called my friend. I ate something and walked another two miles to a member's home. I slept there for two hours. I ate and called my sister-in-law who came and picked me up. At my brother's house now, the phone was taken off the hook so Frederick could not call. I ate again. A couple of hours later Frederick knocked on the door. He said he came for his wife. I obediently got in the car. He of course had all five children along. Joanne was crying; it was time for bed. Back at home Frederick helped bathe and put the children to bed. He asked me where we were to go from here. Never did he ask what led to the events of the day or empathize or apologize for not helping. It was about him. How could I do this to him, leaving him to take care of five children when he had his work to do. I asked if he loved me. He declared that he married me because I would make a fine pastor's wife, helping in the church, and would be a good mother. Nothing about love. Life continued...no changes.

> Be gracious to me, O Lord, for I am in distress; my eye is wasted from grief, my soul and my body also. For my life is spent with sorrow, and my years with sighing; my strength fails because of my misery, and my bones waste away.

> Psalm 31:9-10

I did have a chance to take an evening sewing class at the local high school. I had learned some basics from the lower grade teacher in Cheyenne when I was in ninth grade. But I wanted to make some clothes for the children and for this I needed better skills. Otherwise I purchased all of their attire from garage sales. When I mentioned this class to Frederick he immediately started making phone calls trying to set up a new member instruction class on Monday night, the night I was hoping to take the sewing class. He couldn't find any takers. The Lord blessed me with this one outing. I thoroughly enjoyed the class and being with other women. To appease Frederick who was forced into putting five children to bed, I made him a shirt for my project and did a fine job, thank-you very much. Not long after my class ended Frederick found a good deal on a Bernina sewing machine. I was dumbfounded and thanked him profusely. Well that gesture was ruined when he informed me once again that I should be more grateful to his mother. After all, if she had not given him some money there would be no sewing machine.

One more note on our trip to California. We hit a blizzard in Utah. It was nasty. But Frederick kept driving...surely he wouldn't have to spend money for a motel. He was finally forced to stop when it was a total white out. We finally found a motel room; everyone else had stopped hours before.

My birthday was most often ignored. Another chance for self-pity and resentment. I offer this alternative. Assume there will be nothing and plan your own party. Make yourself your favorite dessert. Invite friends over or ask someone to invite you out. If you are invited out there is a better chance your husband will let you go just to save face. Or buy yourself a present. No, it is not the same but hopefully it will replace sinful reactions to being ignored. It is also important for your children to see you recognized. It won't matter to them that you planned the party. And don't retaliate by ignoring your husband's birthday. In fact go the opposite. Heap coals of fire on his head. Make it a big event. You never know what affect it might have on him. We are called to serve not to be served. Humbling ourselves before God and showing love is different than accepting abuse from our partner.

And there was the rare outing to eat at McDonalds or Pizza Hut. I talked him into a Sunday outing to the park once. We were already to go when a church member stopped in wanting to talk to Frederick about her problems. Frederick put us on hold. The thing was he often talked with this lady. There was no emergency. The problems were the same. Finally we did go but our time was considerably shortened.

Frederick was good in emergencies. We had the inevitable lacerations and had to do the emergency runs. In these instances he was good at helping pick up the pieces of the day and getting back on schedule.

Several times Frederick left the house around 10:00 p.m. without a word. He would return two or three hours later; said he went for a walk. This would be a first; he never went for walks. I knew something wasn't right but couldn't identify it. "Why are you cast down, O my soul, and why are you disquieted within me? Hope in God; for I shall again praise him, my help and my God." (Psalm 43:5) More than a decade later into counseling I asked my sister-in-law what year the church purchased a television for the viewing of church tapes…hmmm, about the same time the *walks* started. This would explain why I could never see him when I searched outside. The church of course was dark.

TEXAS
a respite, hope, reality hits hard

Newsletter - 1982

Change: From short summers and long dry windy winters to long hot summers and short rainy winters. From a modern town of 50,000 to a rural town of 5,600. From a small mission congregation with people from all walks of life to an established congregation of eighty communicants, 90% of whom are related. From a small garden constantly fighting drought and poor soil to both spring and fall gardens that we can hardly keep up with.

We had to leave many friends including Anya's brother and family plus friends dating back to her father's ministry, but we have quickly established new friendships here.

Thomas is in kindergarten...top of his class in math and won a blue ribbon at the County Fair for a water painting.

Paul is the comedian...his mouth gets very little rest. He visited the emergency room for stitches on his knee (third time)

Michael is really a sweet kid, full of questions, who just happens to be all boy!

Marie received a haircut from Thomas…still waiting for two sections to grow out. .still a little mother giving much attention to her *babies* and younger sister.

Joanne puts in a full day learning from her siblings. In November she took a ride on the back bumper of the car for seven blocks before Daddy was alerted to her presence. He thinks twice now before telling Joanne she can't go with him.

We love the beaches though not as clean as California. All but Joanne took swimming lessons. Paul prefers the bathtub.

Anya's father finally made it to Germany. Since then he has gradually been overtaken by his cancer. His strength has been an amazement to all of us.

Anya enjoys her cousin and family in Houston. Frederick has renewed some friendships he had back when he vicared in Houston. Our congregation here is discussing a Christian day school.

Frederick's mother and step-father came to visit in October and enjoyed seeing the South.

Texans love to eat! We have been given everything from beef to pecans, with shrimp our favorite. Frederick spent a day shrimping with one of our members. We are invited often for meals. Their idea of a family dinner is about twenty people.

May the Christchild always have first place in your home because we know that He is the great Giver of all our gifts and to him belongs all the glory and praise.

In order to save money we would pack ourselves. This meant Frederick would pack his study and garage. I continued to take care of five children ranging in age from two years to five years. Somehow I managed to pack a few boxes each day. I was exhausted and wished I had the nerve to pour out my heart to the congregation imploring them for help. Towards the end a lady did ask if it would help to keep the children while I packed. Hurrah! It was so wonderful for the children to have a break. The lady had two grade school age children and a hot tub which ended up putting some premature gray hair on this wonderful lady. As she talked with me on the phone one day she let out a scream and dropped the phone. She returned in a few minutes to explain she could only count four heads; indeed the youngest had gone under but was rescued in time. What fun they had! The packing was completed but there was no time to clean (I heard about this later).

Two men from Texas showed up to load and transport our belongings and they were in a big hurry because by Texas standards it was cold. Of course besides packing I had to plan clothing and meals for seven people for three days. Frederick would want to drive with very few stops and maybe only one or two of those for meals. Games and songs and reading were a challenge. After lunch Frederick would give me a break and let me drive, ha,ha. At first I thought that was really considerate of him until he settled the children down for naps and then he went to sleep. The quiet was nice but then when everyone woke up we stopped at a rest stop and he took over driving. I was tired while the children had renewed energy. Frederick felt great. I wanted to stop early at a motel. He wanted to put more miles on. And so it went each day. We arrived in Texas late in the afternoon. The congregation had set up beds and unpacked as best they could figure out. It was great. We were not there long before some members arrived to welcome us. Supper was brought. Texas was a better life, the best of our married years.

The parsonage was behind the church set off from all other habitation (why do they do that?). One summer day a lady walked from her apartment across the parking lot and lawn and introduced herself as one of the city's kindergarten teachers. She was taken in by my very own preschool class. We became friends. Wow, I had a friend. She brought her three year old over; the children played in water, and we sipped our tea (mine without sugar) and visited; sometimes we played with the children. There were around two hundred members in the congregation, many related, and many of the older generation out in the country. Everyone wanted to visit with *all* of us. They were fascinated with the children and had plenty of land for them to run on plus children and grandchildren for them to play with.

I was excited about a new house…unpacking took forever! But then I had ideas for decorating. The church was willing to make changes for me but Frederick didn't want to burden them. I wanted to paint the dark paneling in one room to lighten it up but he forbid me (guess what the first thing the next pastor's wife did). I was allowed to paint and wallpaper the kitchen and two ladies from the congregation helped me. The linoleum was very old and hard to clean but Frederick would not ask the congregation for this either until one year there was money available from a Lutheran brotherhood insurance company.

This was the beginning of our garden years. Two a year! Large! The ground had to be tilled perfectly. The rows had to be measured. Strings had to be strung. Seeds had to be spaced exactly. I was required to be standing there most of the time while Frederick created these perfect conditions. Of course it was difficult to include the children in this perfectionism. Seeds were checked and extras had to be removed before soil could be patted down. There were no rules for weeding. I could do it however I wanted!!

I was so excited for Thomas, whose brain was overdeveloped, to start kindergarten and he knew his teacher, my friend. I found out she was the best and went to the school early to request her. Frederick actually went with me on Thomas's first day of school. When it came time to leave it was obvious, much to my surprise, that our son was in a panic state. I finally pulled away first, thinking it would be easier for Frederick to leave. It was not. We left him terrified-one of those regretful decisions we have to forever live with. I should have just told Frederick I was staying. I found out from my son when he was grown that it just wasn't a roomful of thirty children but so many of them were black or Hispanic. He was totally scared.

Newsletter – 1983

Christian Day School Opens; Principal Frederick and teacher Jeri are already experienced at their jobs. Eleven children are enrolled.

Heaven Is His Home; After three and a half years of fighting cancer Anya's father has died. Anya attended his *Victory Celebration*. He wrote the service himself as an expression of faith. To symbolize Christ's victory over sin, death, and the devil, he requested a palm leaf with a red ribbon be placed on the casket.

Surgery A Success; After two years of back and forth to doctors, interrupted of course by the move to Texas, Anya finally decided to be done with it. In April she donated her female organs to science (may they finally rest in peace). Recovery was long and slow but tolerable with all the help form the congregation.

Vacation To Wisconsin; Time for a visit to Frederick's family. Anya was given six weeks to regain her strength and off we went leaving Jeri to manage the house and harvest the garden (she says "Never again"). It was funny to watch the corn get smaller everyday as we headed north. Rain followed us everywhere and robbed us of much needed stops to let the kids run. Frederick says there is no need to mention the policeman and how thrilled the kids were that Daddy finally got stopped. They were disappointed he didn't try to outrun the policeman and that he did not get a ticket. We were relieved to arrive at Frederick's brother's home. We swam in a lake, barbecued, and picked strawberries. Next stop was Eau Claire, Wisconsin where Anya went to school. Many happy reunions with people from high school. Next visit was with Frederick's best man's widow. And to Frederick's parents with yet another reunion with relatives. Another lake visit complete with canoes. On the way home three more stops permitted reunions with friends from ages past.

Relatives for Christmas; Anya's mother blessed us with her presence along with her brother, Philip who happened to come the same day. They both experienced bad weather and Philip's luggage arrived via bus twelve hours late. The concern was over the seventy-five pounds of deer and antelope meat he was bringing. His cooking was enjoyed!!

Briefing The News; Frederick finally got out on the golf course a couple of times, and if you care to hear about his 'big shot' you may send a self-addressed envelope for the extra page. Also included will be the details to his new friend, a 1982 Toyota Tercel. Anya had a surprise birthday party from the ladies of the congregation. Having a bad Texas virus did not make any of the food too appealing and she was only good out of bed for an hour.

Highlight: Frederick took Anya out to dinner for their anniversary.

Thomas has figured out that Luther translated the bible into another language so the Pope wouldn't understand it. Paul loves kindergarten and his teacher! He makes funny faces. He received his fourth set of stitches. Michael follows his daddy everywhere and asks an average of 437 questions a day. A cap on his head is his trademark. Marie's average day is highlighted by Bob Barker and a talk on the telephone. Joanne hit a bedpost and knocked out her front tooth. She also cut her hair three days before a scheduled picture.

Bumper Crop; We are still cracking, eating, and freezing pecans. Six tomato plants in spring changed to thirteen in fall. Also added acorn squash and lima beans.

My father was a remarkable man, a great theologian, a loving husband and father. We were very close as I helped run the house even in grade school when my mother worked nights as a nurse. I believe this influenced me in dating. What did I know about *bad* men. I assumed all Christian men would be like my father. And I wanted to be a stay-at-home mother, giving my children the love and attention I saw lacking from my mother. My father had taken over a congregation as an interim pastor. The church body wanted to call someone else but the congregation refused. This was not the church body my father belonged to so he finally made the trip to St. Louis for a colloquy. He expounded to the leaders what was wrong with their church body according to God's word. They opened their arms and welcomed him in. His members dreaded seeing his suffering. He calmly told them he had done his work teaching them to live as Christians now they had to learn how to die as Christians. He even taught the choir *O Come Gentle Death* by Bach. This was another instance where I stood up to Frederick. Siblings were all leaving after the funeral and it was obvious my mother needed someone so I called Frederick and informed him I would be staying a couple days longer. I wish I had learned to make more nonnegotiable decisions.

Some friends from Wyoming days moved to our city. Made a super big difference in my life. At first just the husband moved to establish himself and find a house. Once in a while he would stop over in the evening at the end of his business calls. As Frederick was very seldom home in the evening I visited alone. After the third time this happened Frederick was noticeably agitated upon his friend's departure. I should not encourage his friend to stay. The two of us should not be home alone in the evening. OK, I respected this and soon informed our friend he should call first to see if Frederick was home. The funny thing of this is several times I had dared to confront Frederick about time he spent with women alone, especially one particular teenager. His response was of course it was part of his job but also chided me for my sin of jealousy. I did not know yet that a person with a personality disorder does not connect what the right hand is doing and what the left is engaged in. Finally the wife and children arrived in Texas. The school year provided us time to be together with our four girls or have time alone. I had a friend!

It was also wonderful having a single teacher in my life. I invited her for meals. She was determined to beat me in scrabble.

After my father's death my hormonal dysfunctional body worsened. Ready to crawl into a closet and cry I called my doctor. The same week I had a hysterectomy. Recovery was slow. While I was in the hospital an *adopted* grandma brought meals for Frederick. The children were farmed out. The day after returning home I was in my chair when the children returned home. Not being able to get around much I was surprised to find out the children were much more capable of doing things than I gave them credit for, which was a really good thing because Frederick had vanished. My *adopted* mother was there and knew immediately she would have to return and assist me in my recovery. She made supper and left for the evening. Frederick disappeared again. I was tired and needed help with the children. I finally looked out the back window and there was Frederick going along the fence line around the church property collecting trash. This was a first. I put the children in the bathtub and sat on the floor. Finally he came in as I was drying one off and asked if I needed help! I found out later that the elders had offered to come to the hospital and pray with me. Frederick told them this was not necessary. However, he gave me no spiritual support.

> Thou hast kept count of my tossings; put thou my tears in thy bottle! Are they not in thy book? Then my enemies will be turned back in the day when I call. This I know, that God is for me. In God, whose word I praise, in the Lord, whose word I praise, in God I trust without a fear. What can man do to me? My vows to thee I must perform, O God; I will render thank offerings to thee. For thou hast delivered my soul from death, yea, my feet from falling, that I may walk before God in the light of life.

Psalm 56:8-13

Newsletter – 1984

This year's newsletter will be put out by floundering around on a computer. I'm glad you have all chosen a name for this letter even though they are all different. I am going to be stubborn and stick with New Year's letter just so I keep pushing myself to get started in January.

I have to warn you, this letter may smelt as I believe I reached my peak last year (as in Peter's Principle). As far as anecdotes from the children----either they didn't say anything humorous or my memory is going or I've lost my sense of humor. (It's true, my family thinks of me as an old crab).

PETS; not being a cat or dog lover, my children have been deprived. My guilt and their begging finally drove me to say, "Halibut some chicks?" The neighborhood cats and dogs appreciated the meal. But not to be discouraged I built a cage and bought five more. The cage was not adequate!! Ah, Daddy becomes interested, cannot resist the colored ones at Easter and buys three more. With a little bit of muscle the cage was improved and we did enjoy them for a couple of weeks before they met their doom. Well, a little while later along comes a stray kitten. Smokey seemed to adopt us but after a short stay vanished. One of our members, upon herring the cries of my children, offered us a white kitten, who became Timothy Snowflake, and who also stayed with us only a short time before he longed to see the world. On my behalf I would like to say the aquarium is doing quite well, in fact there is almost constant proliferation.

GARDEN; *Holy Mackerel*, you cannot believe the potatoes and tomatoes last summer. I got so tired of canning I started giving them away by the bagfuls. Cucumbers for pickling were also outstanding. We finally got enough broccoli to freeze and enough cabbage to make sauerkraut.

SCHOOL; Marie is in kindergarten. Luckily we changed to afternoon kindergarten this year or Marie would be outstanding in number of times tardy. I'm sure next year she will still be sleeping at the front door as I snapper up and send her off to school. Joanne attends recess this year.

FAMILY; We saw almost none of you! Frederick's mother and step-father did make it.

VACATION; Had a short rest on Memorial Day weekend north of Houston in a beautiful wooded area with cousins and families; three days, eleven children and not a single fight! Was wonderful to see past friends from WY as well as Anya's brother and family. We had a whale of a time! Took in a few events at *The Daddy of 'em all Rodeos*…the largest outdoor rodeo.

FREDERICK; Had a busy year…new members, second year of school, a paper for this January, working in the garden, learning all there is to know about bicycles, a couple of trips to Milwaukee as circuit pastor and his first funeral shortly before Christmas. Did get to play golf a few times and occasionally enjoys an evening of playing cods with friends. Also makes some fine chocolate chip cookies.

ANYA; Did some sole searching in August and decided it was time to find out about requirements in Texas for a nursing license. So it was off to Victoria every day for a month for an extensive orientation class. It helped to have friend, Marge attend with me. Now I work on call which means they call and I only say yes about three times a month. Do the children mind Mama working? Not at all! Daddy makes cookies and suppers that kids love! Even with four in school I don't seem to accomplish a whole lot more at home yet. Lunches, snacks, homework and teaching some responsibility take the place of diapers and bottles.

THOMAS; His newest interest is German. Personally I wish he would show more interest in a clean room.

MICHAEL; Finally let go of the side of the pool on vacation and found out there is more to do in the middle of the pool. He has the gift of gab and frequently hears, "Michael, clam it!"

PAUL; Not to be outdone several weeks later Paul also ventured out to the middle of the pool. Also not to get too far behind, he finally lost two teeth in Dec. In spite of his outward defiant attitude, he loves hugs and kisses.

MARIE; Loves to tease her Daddy and acts like a girl. Neat and clean however, are not second nature to her.

JOANNE; My little shrimp who thinks she is almost a mother. We enjoy our afternoons together. She informed me the other day that if I had not married Daddy she would have. If you get the feeling I had to do a lot of fishing around to find the contents for this letter, you are right!

The reality of our vacation with cousins was we saw very little of Frederick. Since the children had playmates he spent little time with them. Over the years I was becoming more aware of his desire to admire female bodies. And yes, there he was, on an air mattress, out in the middle of the lake, eyes glued first on one young maiden clad in a skimpy bikini and then on the next. My stomach did flip flops. Was it just me seeing this? A reality check: my cousin remarked on his behavior.

Newsletter – 1985

The highlight for the year was a three week vacation to California. Following is each person's memorable moments.

Daddy; washing windows for my mother-in-law; seeing the Crystal Cathedral including a noon recital on their famous pipe organ; attending the Hollywood Bowl concert with Henry Mancini and James Galway.

Mama; more relaxed and unrushed with three weeks; swimming twice a day and eating my Mother's cooking; the picnic before the Hollywood Bowl performance on the ground complete with fine linen and long-stemmed glasses.

Thomas; we saved our birthday money for Disneyland and it was great; swimming and playing games at Grandma's.

Paul; swimming without water-wings; the electric parade at Disneyland was the best 'cause I got to shake hands with Mickey Mouse.

Michael; Disneyland and swimming without water-wings.

Marie; jumping in the pool; Disneyland; I would like to see my cousin again; I got to sleep in Grandma's bedroom.

Joanne; I liked Grandma's pool and her kitty and the beach and Disneyland and Monique and Uncle Philip is funny.

Personal experiences from this past year:

Daddy; before people started assigning me jobs my desk was clean. I liked having a clean desk! I do enjoy tracking hurricanes. The flood (worst in decades)was exciting; got some good pictures. My mother and father-in-law were out in April. I have lost twelve pounds. Had a wonderful visit with old room-mate and family.

Mama; Made my first solo trip to Houston, taking children to the zoo; managed two camping trips while Frederick was away at conference; worked at the hospital once a week for two weeks then cut back to once every two weeks; quit smoking in October; looking forward to the end of children's *unfunny* joke telling stage; Frederick and I agreed on three issues this year; we worked in the garden for two hours without disagreeing.

Thomas; fishing with my cousin was the best and staying at his place for a week; I love science and I like to read for an hour every night; I love playing piano and games; we made a float for the fair parade. It rained during the whole parade. We took first place in youth division; our entry was Noah's Ark.

Paul; We went camping with our friends not too far from home and saw deer and went fishing and made fires. We bought Daddy a sleeping bag for Christmas in case he can come sometime. I like doing art best at school. I like roller skating.

Michael; I wish my teacher wouldn't give us so much work in second grade, but I did like sitting next to her for piano lessons. I wished it would snow this year like it did last year. We put our coats and boots on over our pajamas and hurried out so we could play lots before it melted. One time a friend pushed me off a truck while we were playing. I had to get three stitches. Mama thought I was Paul until we got to the hospital because he has had stitches four times.

Marie; I can't remember how many cats we've had. They all run away or get killed and so do our bunnies and our chickens. I do fish kisses the best of anyone in the family. I won a coloring contest at a store and got to pick out a toy. I'm learning to read.

Joanne; I like kindergarten, but I wish I could go everyday and do more things. I had stitches last year too; eleven by my chin where Michael hit me with a golf club *"on an accident"*. And I won a coloring contest at a different store. I wish my family wouldn't call me *snoot* anymore 'cause I'm five now.

This concludes our interview.

I was exhausted after Disneyland. We took a motel but I did not sleep well. Next day we went to the beach. Frederick offered to take the children and let me rest. Yes, I was surprised at this seemingly generous show of empathy but soon fell asleep, a very unusual happening for me. When I awoke and my mind was functioning (too bad) I realized the offer gave Frederick a chance without me to do his beach ogling. I'm afraid the children had very little chance to play in the water.

Red letter day…I send Joanne off to school. I watched through the window as she proudly walked to school, lunch box in hand. She would not be five for three more weeks but she was so ready to attend after watching her four older siblings leave. I cried! Thought I would have this sense of freedom but it was an emotional day and I really did not know what to do with myself. And then one day my friend and I went shopping and out to lunch. I would compare it to a day out of jail…awesome but scary. Of course, I was very nervous about being home when the children returned from school lest I exposed myself to Frederick's verbal attacks.

I handled the children's problems at school by myself. Frederick was after all the principal and had to consider his relationship with the teacher. On the good side I was invited here and there by members. I spent some time out in the country doing very hard jigsaw puzzles with a man who was partially paralyzed and in a wheel chair. One of the first times upon being offered food I said should get home. After a little discussion the wife picked up the phone and called Frederick. She informed him I would not be home for a while so he should tend to the children. What could he do?

During my years of child rearing I had let my nursing license lapse. I started thinking what if something happened to Frederick and I had to flip hamburgers to support myself and my children. I checked into steps necessary to activate my license. Not so bad. Had to do in-service in a hospital thirty miles away for a month. Since this would be during school hours and would eventually bring in money Frederick agreed. It was a hard month as I had to catch up on household chores in the evening. There was a discussion on Frederick helping out at home while I was carrying out my recertification and he did actually put in a few hours. Once my license was again active I decided to work Friday evenings. Frederick did not have meetings or calls and I could recuperate on Saturday. Well, this did not last long. The shifts were twelve hours. I arrived home at midnight or later. My legs with varicose veins were painful through Saturday even with support hose at work and surgical hose at night. Even though I had let the hospital know my intended schedule, I was still listed 'as needed'. Many times I received a call at 4:00 a.m. asking me to work the day shift. I shifted down to twice a month and then even to once a month. One night I arrived home to find Frederick and our single teacher in the kitchen cleaning up after donut making. The children of course were in bed. I brought this situation up the next day declaring how their presence together made me feel. I assumed there would be immediate understanding on his part. Had we not gone through this when he was upset with finding his friend with me when he came home? Not so! As usual, I had a problem. I did a reality check with others and everyone sided with me. "Do you suppose, O man, that when you judge those who do such things and yet do them yourself, you will escape the judgment of God? (Romans 2:3)

My birthday often came and went without notice. It was sometimes convenient because the pastor's January conference often coincided with this event. Even though I tried to prepare myself emotionally I was still saddened. One year I decided I would console myself by purchasing my own present. I had long desired a combination mixer/processor. My friend came over on my birthday with well wishes. She asked Frederick what he had given me, ha, ha! My friend looked at me and said, "Well, now you can go buy your mixer." That was all it took. Frederick became irascible. My friend, uncomfortable, left. Knowing Frederick's anger was such that it could very well lead to physical harm I put distance between us ending up on the other side of the dining room table. What a sight, two adults running around a table. When I felt I had enough of an edge, I made for the kitchen door and outside. Still in my bathrobe, I ran to the shed and climbed over a mound of storage. Frederick left me there and returned to the house. I emerged when I thought he had enough time to calm down. No apologies! I did not get my mixer. Two weeks later on Valentine's Day there was a food processor sitting on the kitchen table...*whatever*!

Newsletter (Crescendos And Decrescendos) – 1986

I must caution you to be sharp as you reed this!

Vacation was back to the Michigan/Wisconsin area. While there was typical family dischord along the way we did have moments of quality time together. Frederick reminisced his youth in Michigan and Anya was able to visit relatives and the children were keyed for their boat ride across Lake Michigan. Spent a week with Frederick's mother and step-father. The kids tried their hands at canoeing, finding that an even legato rhythm is the answer.

We found two chances to go camping again. The fun was augmented by including two other family units plus three more children as a favor to a certain Houstonian relative. There seemed to be a large scale departure by other campers soon after our arrival. Six tents later, we all agreed that anyone who says tenting is easy is a lyre. Even Daddy joined us this year (it was not accidental that he received a sleeping bag for Christmas). Ah yes, nothing like an evening campfire with the temperature and humidity both at 85 degrees listening to the concerto provided by owls, egrets and armadillos.

Mom and Dad spent two days together at a missionary/wife conference in Dallas. They learned it does no good to harp at one another.

Anya took her first solo trip…three days to California to spend a little time with her mother. With five kids in school full-time Dad had no problem surviving. At home Anya continues her nursing career to the tune of twice a month. It will be hard to beat last Mother's Day. It was already overwhelming to be presented with card, necklace and a corsage before church. It was too much for all the mothers when the school children, homemade lilies in hand, sang *Consider the Lilies* and then dispersed to present the lilies to their mothers.

Frederick lost thirty pounds and resorted to suspenders (much to the glee of his daughters). Now to improve his muscle tone! Most men don't care for doctors or pain but the pain of a kidney stone is hard to ignore. Frederick chose to faint and have his consultation on the floor of the doctor's office. It was just as well, for the doctor told him, "Duet natural or I'll be forced to get out my instrument." Frederick did make it to his fortieth birthday. It was black except for Anya's red tights. He is taking it well. He lives his life as he taught band…strict timing with particular attention to the rests.

The children of course are above average intelligence and do exceptional things for their age, like taking piano lessons and trying their hands at sports and living day by day in perfect harmony. Of course they all have their little quirks. Thomas practices writing his name many ways in hopes of developing a most appealing signature. Paul feels an interval of silence longer than five seconds is uncomfortable. Michael needs little more than a lawn mower to feel true fulfillment in life. At least he likes to work and won't become a 'oboe. Marie's opera begins ritardando (getting ready for school), gradually moves into a moderato, a very brief allegro and by time to pick up room and do chores is back down to largo. Joanne, the dominant fifth, moves up and down a scale more times in a day than I care to think about. Absolutely nothing is minor in her life.

Thanksgiving Day was spent in Houston with cousins and families times two. Three females on Anya's side of the family were almost enough to drive the men off a clef. And of course everyone goes shopping the day after Thanksgiving so we joined thousands at the Galleria (where not just anyone shops) and rode the escalators and also the enclosed glass elevators to the fourteenth floor (small town people, you know).

We ended the year with a blessed Christmas calling to mind
the angelic choir proclaiming the birth of our Savior.
P.S. New Year's Eve we diminished the fifth!

I came home from work after midnight. Posed, leaning against the counter, almost touching, big smiles pasted on their faces, stood my husband and the grade school teacher. The scene was so vividly absurd, I could not take it in. I ran down to my bedroom. In a few minutes Frederick came into the bedroom and accusingly, told me I had made the teacher uncomfortable.

Pastors in the area convened once a month for "study club." So a couple times a year the meeting would occur at our church. I made sure there was coffee, juice, and donuts at the church. I made lunch at the parsonage. I went back over to the church ahead of the pastors to make sure there was coffee and water for the afternoon. As they entered the church the district president remarked to me that they had been discussing spousal abuse at the end of their lunch. Statistically, he informed me, one out of every five husbands hits his wife. With lightness and joviality, he named off himself and three other pastors who had not struck their wives leaving only Frederick, who therefore must be guilty. Oh, what a grand laugh they had. Too bad they didn't notice Frederick and I were not laughing. What an opportunity I missed.

Trying to plan vacations was a challenge. Frederick did not do well planning ahead. He always made money an issue. But a vacation not totally involving extended family did finally happen. It started out with a gas stop. Gassing up was finished, but Frederick lingered, seemingly writing his mileage down, but there was something not right; his attention seemed divided. On a whim I got out and walked around the van. Gassing up next to us was a young woman provocatively dressed. Frederick's eyes were glued. I was sick to my stomach but just went back to my seat.

We had a wonderful visit with friends in Louisiana. From Louisiana to Chicago virtually every stop involved Frederick's ogling. It was obsessive. Once again I felt on the verge of losing it. A psychiatrist friend once told me concerning another couple that flaunting marital misconduct was the worst form of disregard for a spouse even to the point of hatred. Sometimes I rode in the back just so I would not be able to see where his eyes were focused. He said nothing to me. I didn't exist. In Chicago we visited the Sears tower. He separated himself as soon as we reached the top. I circled around. Now

I was becoming obsessed locating his next victim. He did not disappoint me. I purposely placed myself between him and his ogled victim; he did not catch on. On our way down there was a buxom woman in the elevator, his next object. I again placed myself in his line of view. He shifted, I shifted, and back and forth until he finally realized what I was doing. On the walk back to the van he was livid. What was my problem? I attempted to turn it back to his problem. He was so upset he got lost (he was exceptionally good at directions) and took us into a dangerous neighborhood.

Next visit was in Michigan, my relatives. It was fantastic. Next we crossed Lake Michigan on the ferry. Well, after Frederick had been tied down to family/relative events he was more than ready for ogling adventures and he had lots to choose from. We very seldom saw him. It was extremely difficult for me to forget him and enjoy the children and water. At meal time we all headed down to the van to obtain food we had packed. He positioned and repositioned himself for the best view down a lady's sleeveless blouse. It crossed my mind that I should inform this lady and any others that they were being victimized.

Next was to Frederick's mother. Without children in diapers and able to play alone, I had some time to myself. So, one day I left to get my hair cut. Upon returning I overheard the conversation between Frederick and his mother. His mother was upset at the waste of money. She could have cut my hair. She couldn't even see that much difference in my hair! I also purchased some wine. Since alcohol was firmly regulated I kept it in the back of the van. After the children were in bed I would go out and have a drink and a smoke. This helped Frederick's case later that I was a borderline alcoholic.

Even though my mother-in-law now offered to stay with the children so I could accompany Frederick on his usual outings to visit his friends, he declined to take me. I could have done investigative work. How much time did he actually spend at his friends? But too much information can make life even more miserable.

Then there were the young people who lived next door and left their upstairs curtain open at night. I awoke in the middle of the night to discover Frederick was gone. I heard him come in from outside and asked where he had been. I received one of those generic noncommittal responses. The next morning his niece stated she did not sleep well (on the couch in the living room) because her uncle kept going in and out. It occurred to me the van had been moved and I realized from the driver's side you could see directly in that open window. Was I crazy? Someone was!

The return trip home was more of the same. Settle the children and me in a motel and take off for hours. We were suppose to stop in St. Louis at a dear friend of mine who had planned our day out to make the most of our visit. Frederick said we were not going and that was the end of that. The day after our arrival back home I brought the ogling up and explained how it made me feel. He attacked me verbally for my behavior and unreasonable feelings and explained to me the sexual make-up of men.

> My God, my God, why hast thou forsaken me? Why art thou so far from helping me, from the words of my groaning? O my God, I cry by day, but thou dost not answer; and by night, but find no rest.
>
> Psalm 22:1-2

Most of my time during those grade school years was taxiing children to practices and attending events. One baseball game was attended by Frederick. I spied him on the opposite end of the field from where I was sitting. He stayed a short while and left. He did attend piano recitals, I think because in a smaller group it would be noticeable if he was absent. He was guided by what other people would think.

Michael was premature in that his twin brother shunted his blood away for an undetermined number of weeks. He was immediately given a blood transfusion. I mention this because he had a hard time grasping basic concepts already in first grade. Time had to be spent with him every afternoon/evening helping him complete his homework. To God be the glory. What we look at as humanly impossible, God is able to accomplish through our prayers and faith. Michael is the only one to complete post graduate education.

Newsletter – 1987

ACAPULCO! Magnificent…a second honeymoon…
Camelot…a taste of heaven! A week of delicious meals cooked

by Fide. Poolside service from Alfredo. Spotless rooms thanks to Angelina. A thousand thanks to friends of Anya's parents.

BASEBALL games and practices added that *new dimension* to our lives.

CHILDEN are all doing well in school and passed MY summer program of learning to do more around the house. They all want to bake…oh, that they could get the same thrill out of cleaning toilets!

DETECTIVE Frederick they call him! First it was my billfold, stolen out of my purse in the car parked in front of a friend's house. "They would try to get rid of the billfold as quickly as possible, I'm sure. All they wanted was the money," Frederick speculated out loud. So off we went to check the bushes and dumpsters. Five minutes and three dumpsters later, there it was! What a relief! Then there was his cross stolen out of the sacristy. Off goes detective Frederick to the neighboring apartments to a young girl from the church to see if she had heard any talking. She had pertinent information and yes, he tracked it down although there never was a firm conviction.

EASTER brought the assurance of our sins forgiven and the assurance that heaven is ours. May we unite to bring more ideas for our home and churches to make Easter the festive celebration it should be. We are on our own. The world offers nothing but chicks and bunnies.

FAIRY TALES were acted out for the school *Spring Thing*! Marie seemed to strongly resemble 'someone' when she played the mother of the three little kittens. Joanne truly believed she was a queen in *Four and Twenty Blackbirds*!

GALVESTON was not Acapulco but hey, it was stupendous! Some members lent us their beach home. Hours were spent on the beach and going back and forth on the ferry (a fifteen minute ride each way), complete with dolphins. Was amazing to see a ship from the Soviet Union docked in the bay. Anya took in the history of Galveston and the great hurricane while the children watched a movie at the library and Frederick read up on fixing lawnmowers. We also took in Sea World.

HORSE-back riding was a first for the children. It started with a bicycle outing and a stop at an acquaintance for a drink. Soon two horses were out and rides were given. Marie took a spill and Anya lost a couple of years as she helplessly watched the front hoof coming down on a knee. But contact was not made. Well, I went to Cheyenne to find me a cowboy but took a minister instead, or so I thought. You should have seen him ride...! Yes, I took my turn, but the old gray mare just ain't what she used to be.

INFECTION from the '86 kidney stone did not deter the cowboy, detective, theologian from making the Arizona conference. After notifying the doctor, he was on his way, stopping just long enough for a prescription. What dedication!

JANE, our teacher deserves honorable mention (because most likely she will be reading this and I'm going to send a copy to her parents). Besides being a blessing to our school and congregation, it is personally gratifying to have someone help me keep Frederick in line.

KEEP in touch!

LESSONS in the way of piano continue for Thomas and Marie. Joanne, who always has to be last, finally gets her turn. I work with Michael and Paul a little at home. Ministry presents a good share of challenges. There were an unusual number of baptisms during the year, both children and adult, some from an entire family.

NURSING still plays a small role in Anya's life...has been three years!

OUTDOORS tenting during spring and fall vacation still remains a big a family favorite (right, Frederick?). Well, the kids like it!

PETS seem to be a *must* with children. Fish are still doing well. We have added a parakeet.

QUIET is my favorite word!!

RECITATIONS in Houston for a Forensic Meet was attended by Thomas. A great opportunity to fellowship with the other Christian Day Schools.

SPELLING bee gave three of our school children a chance to compete. While no one placed in the city finals, Marie walked away with a trophy for beating out the other two (older boys) in our school.

TROPHIES are great! Our float entry in the Fair Parade took first in Youth Division – that's two out of three years.

UNLESS unforeseen happenings occur, God willing, we will vacation in Cheyenne at Hynds Lodge this July.

VACATION quickie to Wichita Falls in June was most enjoyable. Brother Dan, wife, and four girls were visiting relatives so we intruded.

WOLTMANN as in Grandpa and Grandma visited in March. Actually, they stayed with some of the children while we bathed in the sun and luxury of Acapulco.

XTRA visit with brother Dan when business brought him to Houston.

YULETIDE came and went without snow. The Christchild's birthday was properly celebrated as best we poor mortals can do. Yours truly did the children's program this year.

ZEALOUSLY we enter the new Year, blessed with good health and more than adequate material blessings, eager to carry out the Lord's work…for is there any other reason we are here?

Acapulco was one of the best times Frederick and I had together. Of course it helped that it cost nothing except the flight. At our wedding reception this friend of my father said that if Frederick could stand me for ten years he would have us down to his place in Acapulco. He and his wife were on my newsletter mailing list so when I sent the newsletter following our tenth anniversary I made reference to his promise never expecting he would follow through. He called after receiving my newsletter and asked when we would like to come. I doubted Frederick would agree; he said to put him on the phone. He gave Frederick two choices of dates and said to call him back in five minutes. And so we were off.

But even this trip was tainted. About the third day Frederick caught a ride into town. He did not encourage me to come along. Late in the afternoon we began to wonder why he was not back. Finally he showed up with a noticeable gash on his knee. He had spent the afternoon walking the beach. I was no longer naive. I knew what the attraction was (he was not a beach person). Nobody knew him and there would be hundreds of bikinis to choose from. The beach was long, so instead of back tracking he climbed the rocks to our abode, slipping when he had to jump from one rock to another, thus scraping his knee. We had many intimate moments in our room but I just wasn't enough for him.

Even though we again did fairly well at Galveston, Frederick took advantage of ogling scenarios. I went alone to learn the history of Galveston because he just plain and simple did not want to go with me.

The camping became very routine. I packed; we drove to the campsite; Frederick helped put up the tent; he spent meal times with us; he either slept in the van (alone) and went home after breakfast to shower or just slept at home.

I thought he would attend the Forensic Meet in Houston, what with other pastors and their families attending, but no, he wasn't interested.

I had to fight for all of the children's outside activities. Frederick was good at sports and music so it never made sense to me that he fought against his children being involved. All I could figure was that it was the money.

> See that none of you repays evil for evil, but always seek to do good to one another and to all. Rejoice always, pray constantly, give thanks in all circumstances; for this is the will of God in Christ Jesus for you.
>
> I Thessalonians 5:15-18

Newsletter – 1988

Frederick: Trips to Milwaukee for CCFS…has moved up to carburetors and engines
Is very good at square dancing

Anya: Spending more time at church and school, less time dusting…working as nurse once/mo. instead of twice…will never again have 3 boys on 3 different baseball teams.

Frederick & Anya: Went on a trip to South Padre Island, Mexico, and Harlingen

Thomas: Becoming more interested in sports and computers…entered steer riding Competition at state fair…was too scared to let go and came in first…went to *Beach Boys* concert with Mom and Dad.

Michael: Was on 1st place team in baseball…also entered steer riding claims his mother *needs* him…loves money.

Paul: Loves doing homework…working on being in shape… acquiring more depth in his rhetoric ..admits he loves his mother.

Marie: Taking up cross-stitching…on to diving lessons… cooperates on occasion by completing her assigned tasks…

Joanne: Lost for 2 hours at carnival in Cheyenne…authority on fashion…expressing her exuberant personality in creative writing.

Family: Children help more with packing for camping…trip to Cheyenne for reunion on Anya's side…two noteworthy stories follow.

The Hunt

Eleven cousins aging from 3 to 12 years old went on a rabbit hunt in the mountains. They were armed with a small bow and arrow, slingshot, and sticks. The poor defenseless bunny was cornered and killed. After an anatomy lesson by their Uncle Philip down at the creek, the bunny was sautéed and served up as an "hors de ourve." Not a queasy stomach among them!

Rat Patrol

> One evening as we sat around visiting a rat was spied sticking his head out from behind the refrigerator. My brother who spied him had served in Vietnam and said he was out of there. My other two brothers jumped at the chance to eradicate this monster. My older brother lit a cigarette and threw it under the refrigerator to smoke him out (later Frederick would tell that the rat threw the cigarette back out). Next was camphophenic applied to a fly swatter. This the rat did not like and as he emerged my younger brother was waiting with fireplace harpoon poised and the kill was made!

For all the time Frederick could not spare for me or family he found hours upon hours to work on his vehicles. The good thing about it was Michael and Paul loved being involved with this. Also, I must say that we had very few auto problems.

Square dancing was the best family time we ever spent together. Why did Frederick join in on this? It was taught by members at the church with other members taking part. The Cheyenne vacation was also great. It was just us in the mountains...no side attractions! Frederick was forced to take part in family activities.

Newsletter - 1989

January brought one of our families worst sicknesses. All five children took turns with high fevers missing one week of school except Paul who started it off during vacation. Anya entered the forties' world with a diamond from the spend-thrift Frederick. I resolved to exercise and did well for several months. Cold and Ice for Ash Wednesday!

February was spelling bee (Marie..another trophy) and forensics competition in Houston.

March another campout. *April* Thomas acquires a lawn job. *May* was baseball, the school play and piano recital. In *June* Paul learned to whistle and we harvested a 9#, 24" circumference cantaloupe! In *July* Anya and Frederick flew to Michigan for Frederick's 25th high school reunion. Also visited Anya's relatives.

Had a day alone in Frankenmuth. In *August* our new teacher and his wife arrived. They and some friends went with us to Padre Island. We took a couple of days visiting New Braunfels (water slide and river tubing), LBJ ranch (with Raindrops keep falling on my head playing during the tour) and Fredricksburg where we observed candle making. On our way home we picked a peck of peaches. In *September* Paul and Michael were put back on the piano to compliment their baseball interests. Anya took computer classes at the hospital. Thomas begins baritone lessons at local Junior High (instructor chuckles at Dad's OLD baritone). *October's* campout was a lesson in the reality and severity of the ten plagues. School float entry, "Fishers of Men" takes 2nd place. Thomas ties for 2nd in steer riding. Frederick has another meeting in Milwaukee and reunion with his family. Ahhh, *November*...Anya is in bed for 3wks with the flu..3 weeks more to recover and 2 relapses yet after that. Dance recital for girls (tap, ballet & jazz). They did well & I have done my thing for that phase of life. Amen. Children enter local coloring and pumpkin carving contests. Enough wins to pay for half of a Nintendo. *December* brought a Hard Freeze...will set palms back 3 years. Brother, wife and four girls come for Christmas. What a riot! What fun! What a lot of kids! What a wonderful Christmas! December 31st, Joanne came down with the chicken pox...to be continued!

The Lord gave us more than our share of blessings for the year and just enough hardship to keep us looking to him and toward heaven, knowing we will never find any lasting happiness her on earth. To him be all praise and glory.

P.S. 29 days into the New Year we said goodbye to Anya's brother, Philip. The Lord took him quickly and painlessly only five days before his 38th birthday.

A few words about Frederick's 25th high school reunion: sometimes he introduced me but mostly I was just a quiet (who me quiet?) side kick. There was one woman who all but threw herself at him. Extremely obnoxious! In looks and demeanor she was (I kid you not) the spittin' image of his mother. She even ruined the formal dinner by choosing to sit at our table. Frederick went along with it all. We slept in single beds in the dorm. Oh, did I mention when the reunion was first brought up I was not included in the trip?

By our trip to New Braunfels his ogling had become even more of an obsession with me. I couldn't let go. I looked ahead preparing myself for who would capture his interest. I had no intention of subjecting myself to all the women at the water slide and therefore chose tubing down the river. Thomas and Marie also wanted to be a part of this. It was really hilarious because the river was moving so slow we actually had to hand paddle to make any progress.

A very sad day arrived the day after my birthday. I received the call that my younger brother had died. He had been electrocuted while cutting down trees on my mother's property in northern California. My mother had discovered him on the ground with one arm burnt. Frederick was in a meeting at church. I called, barely able to communicate the news. In thirty seconds a couple, not Frederick, was at the house just to be with me. I was touched immensely by this act of empathy. Frederick did make flight arrangements and took me to the airport the next morning. A word about my brother: he served in the army in Turkey. He had top clearance on the base and so rubbed shoulders with those in charge. In this way he learned there was diamond smuggling going on. Being a good citizen he started bringing a tape recorder and camera to work to obtain proof of the smuggling. One day on the way back to his barracks he was tapped on the shoulder and told not to turn around. He was told that if he did not give up his investigation he would be given leave, drugs would be planted on him, and the Turkish police would be informed. He would be arrested, put in prison and no one would hear from him again. He panicked and called home. My father was at a loss what to do. Finally he thought of the Red Cross, called and told them his wife was distraught over her son's mental state. The Red Cross amazingly called back that same day and said he would be on a flight home. We were called the next day and informed he failed to catch one of his connecting flights but they would track him down. By this time my brother was in an acute schizophrenic state with severe paranoia. He had stayed on his first plane convinced people would be waiting as he disembarked the plane to get rid of him for what he knew about their diamond smuggling. The Red Cross informed us they had lost him. They found him again; he was on a plane to New York. When he disembarked in New York he spied two "suits" and quickly gave them the slip. They of course were Red Cross workers. He ended up at a policeman's house…who knows how that happened. Eventually he was on a plane heading home. When my father, mother, and I met him at the airport he buried his head on my mother's shoulder and wept. After two days of bizarre behavior we admitted him to the veteran's psychiatric unit. The long and short of it is he recovered but with some emotional changes which were good and bad. His sense of humor over his mental state kept us all in stitches.

There was so little that transpired smoothly around my brother's funeral. There was stress, stress, and more stress. There were some long overdue sibling talks that did come out of it and that was good. Some of this sharing took place at a local bar. Sadly I was exposed to the smoking of three relatives and so after having quit for one year, I was once again hooked. It was difficult coming back home. I experienced the same let down as I had when my father died. Being with people who never met the deceased gives you no one to really continue your grief process with. In bed that first night, I was still relating facts from my trip. I admitted I was smoking again. What was I thinking? Did I really believe due to the stress of the situation Frederick would understand? This is so typical. We feel a little love, a little understanding, and we think we have attained some normalcy in our relationship. Frederick exploded!! Emphatically he stated he better never catch me smoking. Welcome back to reality!

A few months later Frederick accepted another call 1000 miles north of us. Once again there was packing. At least the children were older and could help. And another farewell party. These I enjoyed. I think it was because the attention was not just on Frederick but on our family as a whole. I felt a unity that for the most part was missing in our marriage. Farewells with these individuals was very difficult.

NEBRASKA
depression, porno, health

Newsletter (Almanac) - 1990-1991

Preface: Since this is not a newsletter there will be no opening list of excuses for being late or for not publishing an item last year. There will also be no closing paragraph of apologies for the length of the "book." Chapter titles are listed so you won't be coerced into reading uninteresting or overrated material. As my dear departed brother, St. Philip, always said, "There are a lot of things some of us aren't interested in."

Chapter 1…Texas
Chapter 2…Nebraska
Chapter 3…Famous People
Chapter 4…Achievements
Chapter 5…Medical
Chapter 6…Vacations
Chapter 7…Trivia

Acknowledgements; To my family without whom I would have no excuse to compose; to extended family and friends who touch our lives in ways worth writing about; and to the faithful readers who must be hard up for reading material!

TEXAS

We will not easily be able to forget our Texan ways – 9 years is a long enough time to determine some cultural change and of course for the children…they basically know nothing else. The memories are countless : the gulf Galveston, Barbecues (well-done hamburgers), pecan orchards, gardens (host of bugs), Houston, Mexico, Padre Island, El Paso (over-sized grasshoppers), spelling bees, baseball games, San Antonio, 'The Hill Country', our Christian Elementary school. And so in June we said farewell with an overwhelming endless list of tearful farewells.

NEBRASKA

April 2nd.. the call came. May 5th Frederick accepted. June 13th we arrive in Wilber. A two story home and church complete with steeple and bell, a school behind and a church cemetery, all four miles west of Clatonia. The president and his wife went out of their way to welcome us and help us settle in, even apologizing for the high humidity! June 14th the moving van arrives and after several fun filled family unpacking days, we left for Wyoming. We returned July 2nd to spend the summer organizing, learning names and faces, checking out towns and cities and learning about farm life. With two churches, Frederick had plenty of work. Weddings and funerals did not wait for him to be comfortably settled in. Anya and Children were able to visit Nebraska City from which you can cross the wide Missouri and be in three states in less than an hour. The boys took up cross country biking doing up to 30 miles in one day. They were also able to do some field work and a gun left for their use by their uncle opened up a new avenue of life. Along with another family they provided a meal of pheasant, quail and rabbit. The girls also did some biking, planted a flower bed and became the proud owners of two kittens. Anya feels she has now completed her 'circle of life' having started in Gresham and returning to within 60 miles of her birthplace. Thomas attends our Lutheran high school in Waco. A rigid school and dorm life has been a hard adjustment but we are confident he will get it together by graduation. He works in the kitchen and makes it home about once a month. The others have 18 children (grades 4-8) in their room and have much homework! They attend public school several times a week for band. We are content with rolling hills of wheat and corn in summer and refreshing, invigorating snowfalls in winter.

FAMOUS PEOPLE

We have had sooo many visitors! Some from Cheyenne, our hosts from Acapulco, our nanny, Frederick's relatives for his installation, and friends from Texas. Our last year in Texas Anya's mother spent six weeks with us and the encounter was nontraumatic! She helped us lose weight but our growing collops need her back! Sadly, an elderly lady in Texas whom Anya had helped and given cancer shots three times a week for a year, died two weeks after we left Texas. We were unable to attend the funeral but look forward to seeing her in heaven. Also our dear friend in Cheyenne died. We were able to attend his funeral. And my sister for whom this chapter was actually titled, has published a book, "A Man without words", through publishers, Simon and Shuster. It tells of her personal experience with a deaf man. If you have seen "Awakenings", the names Oliver Sack and Dr. Sayer, both instrumental in Susan writing her book, will be familiar to you.

ACHIEVEMENTS

Frederick is able to play golf, baseball, basketball and volleyball now that we are in an area with many pastors and a larger congregation. He is also the proud owner of a '78 Mercedes. Anya produced the 500th anniversary Martin Luther play. Had help from several devoted mothers and outstanding work from the grade school children. She now plays in a monthly bridge club and substitutes in a weekly club. She also earned a 5 year pin at Citizens Hospital, ignoring all the snide comments about her total number of days worked. One year later she was fired when some aereopagus decided not enough weekend hours had been worked?? She is back to helping in school with spelling and math facts. She also walked/ran a 2 mile race in Lincoln for the arthritis foundation. The boys are all anxious to be behind a wheel especially when they spend so much time with the farm kids who drive trucks, etc. For right now they must be content to start the vehicles and practice turning in the driveway (they put on an amazing number of miles). Thomas graduated 8th grade and was confirmed in Texas. Marie was exposed to the arts with the rest of her 6th grade English class. Teacher treated them to a catered meal of shrimp and then to a performance by an acclaimed Chinese dancing group. The girls accompanied the 'Ladies' to a 'Living Christmas Tree' concert in Lincoln. A word for parochial education…when our school closed and the children transferred to public school, they were placed in advanced classes and ended up on the honor roll and high honor roll.

MEDICAL

Sorry to have left you hanging for two years wondering what happened after Joanne manifested the chicken pox on New Year's Eve! Well of course, the others all followed, Marie, then Thomas who was older than one should be and so had a severe case with many scars. Paul and Michael followed with hard but not severe cases and so ended January…life could only improve…except we hadn't made an emergency run for stitches in quite some time so Thomas caught us up. February was flu month and I think it was then I decided the yearly update just wasn't going to happen. More measles inoculations and sport physicals (now there's a profiteering enterprise) and 10 year tetanus boosters…Paul had his early as he initiated himself to Nebraska and pig farming by cutting himself across the chest on a barb wire fence! Had a nasty virus before Christmas. Marie had the record breaking fever of 105.2, Joanne came in second with 104.6 and while 103 would normally get me moving it hardly seemed worthy of too much extra attention for the boys. And while being a gracious hostess, butter flying partially thawed lamb chops, Anya cut through to her hand…to the tune of 4 stitches in 2 different places. Oh yes, Frederick was sick a few times too…*sicker than anybody else has ever been before*!!!!!

It amazes me we have made it into the teenage years with no broken bones!!!

VACATIONS

Our last summer in Texas we left for the "The Hill Country" starting in San Antonio at the "Lone Star Brewery". Ate out with local pastor and wife…great margaritas! Next morning we intended to follow the scenic route west, missed it, but got directions in Uverde to Con-can where we enjoyed an absolutely beautiful breathtaking day in actually mountainous type country and inner-tubed down the Guadalupe soaking up the sun. After leaving there we accidentally found Garnet State Park where the children took a hike and we had a picnic supper. At 8 pm we ended up in Kerville and were ready for a motel but there were none to be had…there or anywhere…some sports playoffs going on. As we trucked northward the lights on the van seemed to be less bright and change intensity or could it just be our imagination? No! 10pm found us on the side of the road with a broken alternator belt. Since the last time a belt broke on the way to Houston, Frederick had purchased several to keep in the van but not the right size for this occasion. Half an hour later a highway patrol stopped and stayed with us for two hours. Finally the tow truck took us in to Buerney where again there was no room in the inn so they towed us to an all night truck stop and we cozily settled down in the van (Yuk!!). Next day was Sunday but in a small friendly town people go out of their way to help. A traveling fix-it-all put us back on the road for an unheard of cheap price. Things could only improve after those cricket filled showers and not much breakfast as our mishap had eaten up our cash. On to Fredricksburg, a clean motel, showers, food and sleep! Next day we took in the "Enchanted Rock", went climbing and toured the Nimitz museum. Great browsing in quaint German shops. Next morning we picked several bushels of peaches and left for Austin. Visited the capitol and on the way home stopped at a roadside park for a *cold* swim in a spring fed pool. Our 1991 trip to Wyoming gave us a chance to see many friends and of course Anya's brother and his family who would soon be moving to Rock Springs. Through one of his business associates we spent several days in Pinedale in an absolutely beautiful mountain home. It had been twenty years since Anya had been to the favorite family vacation spot.

Directing the Martin Luther play was a great and rewarding joy for me. Luckily I got the teacher and former teacher on my side or Frederick would have forbid me on the grounds it was too much of an undertaking. The children loved it. Frederick, as principal of the school, introduced the play…sounded like he had contributed and offered support. He gave me no credit. However, I was presented with a bouquet of flowers at the end by the students and teachers.

Our marriage was now rocky at best. Always interested in saving the church money we would pack up ourselves. This meant he would do his study and outside and I would do the rest while taking care of five children. I anticipated an emotionally distressing trip complete with his obsession of ogling women. There would also be late night trips by Frederick under the auspice of filling the car with gas and buying groceries for the next day. It would do no good to question him on how this could take hours. Anyway, how could I take a chance of awakening his angry side and exposing my children to his raving. He of course played on my motherly protectiveness. I had little sleep, first waiting for him to return to the motel long after midnight and then imagining possible explanations; a bar, maybe a strip bar, an x-rated movie. It was perfect for him being in a town where no one knew him. Traveling, I tried to avoid where his eyes may be roving but it was almost impossible. These were extremely depressing days for me. I was totally controlled and manipulated by circumstances providing me no escape.

At last, arrival in Nebraska meant he would now behave and put on a good act for his new members. We received a grand welcome but I remember I was barely responsive which is totally unlike me. He became busy with his study and visiting new members. I had a house to set up. It was an old house with bedrooms upstairs where the children would be.

I have never forgiven myself for a change I made in night time routine with my children. I had always spent some time with each of them after they were in bed, ending with prayer and a hug. It was physically more than I could extend myself to climb those stairs yet one more time in the evening. At first I had them come down for a quick goodnight but that deteriorated to a verbal goodnight.

The four children were not happy in their church school but their father, always more interested in church people's feelings than his children prevented me from trying to communicate with their teacher, who was extremely rigid with 'rules' and totally unimaginative in his teaching.

Smoking was now a challenge, as it was on the trip, since he had forbid me to smoke. The house was on a main highway, the church right next door and the school behind. The only cover I had was back in the tree line by the church cemetery. I had to choose my times wisely making sure the coast was clear. In winter, well, I actually gave up a few rather than winterize myself for the walk. Sometimes I hung outside the upstairs bathroom window just enough so the smoke wouldn't come back in. The angle was just right so as not be seen from the school.

Thomas was ahead in math which I conveyed to his high school teacher. I found out a few weeks later that she indeed had not advanced him but stuck him in the regular ninth-grade class. He was bored! Frederick was not interested.

Now began the years of Frederick lashing out at the children. Actually, the first incident was the last year in Texas. Thomas, after some smart remark, was cornered in the laundry room and slapped back and forth. He came to the supper table with a swollen lip. Paul was next. The incidence took place during supper. There was an argument between Frederick and Paul. Finally Frederick told him that was enough. He continued. I still do not understand his lack of obedience in this. Then Paul was told to leave the table. He did not. Finally Frederick grabbed him from his seat, lifted him off his feet, held him against the wall and proceeded to slap him back and forth. You want to do something but the surprise just leaves you frozen to your spot. Finally Frederick let him go and he ran upstairs to his room. All I could do was go upstairs, give him a hug, tell him I was sorry that I did not stop it, and promise to not let it happen again. The most amazing thing is that Paul does not remember this event.

Newsletter - 1992

This is an attempt to make sausage story as you have never read. Sow here goes. Maybe I'll get this litter out in record time.

Poor Thomas...the year started out poorly when he backed the Mercedes out of the garage making the turn a little too soon and a little too sharp. He has recovered from his misteak due to his famous motto, "I don't allow any stress in my life." However, his father's stress level was definitely elevated!

Anya was able to attend a few of Thomas's track meets to watch Thomas hoof it 100 yards and a ½ mile. There was also the grade school track meet at the high school. Our grease lightning children even took some first and seconds.

The children all had their first chance to play on an organized basketball team. Paul even made a three pointer!

Anya is still trying to get to Washington, D.C. via the girl's spelling talents. Marie took the school spelling bee, but it was Joanne who went from County to District.

Our big event of the year was confirmation for Michael and Paul and their 8th grade graduation.

The spring and summer rains were so abundant that wallowing in the mud was not a problem. In spite of the wetness the boys loined much about farming and indeed brought home the bacon. Thomas started as a dishwasher at a family (church members) owned restaurant where his mother also worked as a waitress. He quickly moved up to Mexican entrees (2nd time he worked) and fast food cooking. They like him better than his mother so I quit. Paul spent any time he wasn't working for other farmers, over at his friend's house working for them, farming and slopping hogs, often hock deep in____! The girls found some piglets to baby-sit. There were times of udder chaos keeping track of jobs and mealtimes.

Do not think the poor children labored all the time. There was baseball and basketball and swimming. Paul and Michael enjoyed leisure time outside with guns shooting poor defenseless creatures of God's creation. There was also a week's vacation in Wisconsin. Hogust was historical and hysterical equipping three to leave for High School. After their departure it was quiet, it was strange…the girls loved It! All three boys started out with a week of football camp. They played left shank, tail end and hind back. Mother squealed with delight when Thomas made his first catch. Michael was elected to student council. He has mellowed and taken his place in the ranks since he called a fellow student a sowbelly and received a knuckle sandwich. Sometimes it just doesn't pay to butt heads! Paul had to change stalls a couple of times but is settled in. It took most of Sowtember to realize that hamwork had to be done on time! Michael and Paul have tried out the game of dating. They both have taken quite a bit of ribbing.

And there is still music. Thomas surprised us by trying out for the smaller tour choir. We didn't even know he could oink. We do enjoy all of the choir and band concerts. It is exhilarating to hear young adults sing, especially in praise to our Lord. The tour choir will be on the road the end of Hamuary. Joanne is on the clarinet, Marie on flute, Michael on coronet and Paul and Thomas on baritone. Thomas, Marie, and Joanne also take piano. Mother frequently snorts about practice, they grunt back and all in all we have a swill time. Those of us who are into culture attended *Oliver* in Lincoln's outdoor theatre and heard The United States Marine Band on tour. Those of us interested in fitness (Anya, Michael, Marie and Joanne) ran in the 2 mile *Jingle Bell Run*. Our treat afterwards was porking out at the

Village Trough, compliments of Bob, a renowned long distance runner.

It may be time to face the truth. As boaring as it may be reading about each other's kids… without them we would have nothing to write about.

Besides his weekly sermon study, Frederick is busy with weddings, funerals and hospital calls. He usually finds himself shoat on time, even has to give up some afternoons in the blanket. He is becoming proficient on the computer though he still has to check with Thomas now and then.

Anya is still at home writing silly letters, chewing the fat and feeling just gilty enough to check out a job possibility every month or so. She accepted the chair position for worship for the '93 church women's convention in Sioux Falls. But by far her biggest challenge is on the weekends changing dormitory manners (?) instantaneously upon arriving at home. Rooting in your plates, chewing with jowls open and smacking your chops are forbidden!!!

Other than that we just stay busy chewing our way through the gristles of life, butting heads with each other, all too often swining about our wurst burdens that can't be cured and now and then knuckling down with snouts to the grindstone.

One word about my hammy sister, Sooey! Her book, *A Man Without Words* has been published in England and Germany, and in paperback. The movie is still on a warm burner…having trouble in Hollywood with the script writer (don't we all).

So much for intellectual pig latin! Stay tuned for more "Spam the news" next year.

Did I mention we had more tomatoes from Jowly to Octailber than we knew what to do with? And Marie and Joanne's room is not a pig pen…they spent days arranging it that way! Michael could chop every day for week and still ask us the next day if we are going to Lincoln or Omaha! Oh spare me, my ribs ache from laughing!

I hope you can come up with a more original comment than "This stinks!"

Our first year I just assumed Frederick and I would attend high school events together. Guess I'm a slow learner, forever hopeful. Discussion of course did not work. He could always say his ministry demanded his time. And so I began the first of many years attending the children's high school activities on my own. The first few times the children and other parents asked where he was but soon it was just accepted he did not attend events except for concerts. The upside of him not attending with me was I could stop halfway at a quick stop and have a cigarette.

Before school began again Frederick nervously paced and grumbled about the tuition, now for three children. Finally, he said it – I should get a job. After all I was finding some time to be with other women and wasting all that time at the high school. And so I ended up being a waitress for the first time in my life at a friendly small casual restaurant owned by a church member. My first night back home I brought in all of my dollar tips and strew them across the bed with an attitude of, there, I hope you're happy. He didn't care about my attitude...he was happy. As it turned out I very much enjoyed the bantering with customers, many of them from our church.

Everywhere we lived the Lord saw to it that I had some friends to carry me through my dismal married life. We are tested but the Lord provides a way out. I did not confide my problems to these friends (after all he was their pastor) but they lightened my load and also the children's.

Newsletter – 1993

First and foremost as I frantically fight to find a format for this flamboyant newsletter...we are fine, the weather is freezing (especially my feet) with occasional snow flurries. Yes, we had plenty of rain, area rivers flooded, even our field during a funnel cloud warning during which the fearless (?) men took pictures for following generations! Actually I wanted to do the "Top Ten Reasons" why I love teenagers but that idea was stolen by femme fatale feiffer (h.s. buddy).

Relax now and take your time to filter through these frivolous details of our life on the frontier. Warning: there may be slight fabrications!

Frederick flitted back and forth to Wisconsin/Michigan, first as a delegate to the convention in Saginaw and then for his step-father's funeral. He has a new hobby...observing finches from his study desk where just outside he has placed a finch feeder. He has also had to start a new file folder for secretary of our Lutheran High School. Affirmative…he still finds time to fix his cars.

Anya's female human parent tarried yet another six weeks following Christmas, 1992. She now hangs out in Alpine, Wyoming with Anya's brother.

Anya had a fabulous time at her first women's convention in Sioux Falls. Besides chairing the worship committee she also flaunted across the stage in her fleeting stage career as one of the famous *Nebraska Bluebells* (tape available for small fee). Is it a fluke that occasional job opportunities that pop up always have something to do with food service? Besides waitressing, which has fizzled out, catering and helping in the high school kitchen have presented themselves. Anya is also involved at the high school as 1st vice president of the Ladies' auxiliary.

We are truly fortunate to be able to send our children to our Lutheran high school where Christian fundamentals are fostered, forming a firm foundation, yet have them home on Friday and take part in so many of their activities, the greatest being their concerts. We never tire of seeing and hearing the young people play and sing using their talents to the glory of God!

Thomas turned sixteen and along with his brothers took driver's education. For fysical fortification the trio took karate augmented with weight lifting. They still found over forty hours a week to work for farmers and food service.

Facts and figures have brought Thomas some fame. He placed third in math competition at school allowing him to be a part of the team to conquer first place at the University of Lincoln Math Day. He also was a high scorer in New Ulm Meet Math, the Juniors/Seniors taking a first place for the third year in a row!

Feuds of the filial type resound on weekends over piano practice time. Michael who became frustrated with fingering the keys in fourth grade has once again resumed lessons, likewise Paul.

Michael literally flew the coop with a helicopter ride upon spending a weekend with a friend from school…yes, he flinched! While wrestling wouldn't be mother's choice, it seemed futile to object to this new interest of Michael's.

The frugal financial pair (Michael and Paul) not only work furiously during summer but continue during the school year, running their private stores from their dormitory room closets. They are good patrons of Sam's. Free enterprise is alive! Fortunately for our fine feathered feasants, Paul only fired on a few frenzied roosters. Beware O Fox and Fowl! His fame is being on the honor roll. His motto is "Be an Overachiever." All three weekend fuzz shavers fumbled their way through football camp!

Marie and Joanne no longer have felines but have gone back to fish, would you believe Ferdinand, Fanny and Fred??? It's feasible!

Marie was confirmed in May (in spite of friction over the frock) with Frederick's mother and niece attending. As a fair freshman she found favor with enough classmates to be featured in the 'homecoming court'. She and her sister convinced their brothers to fork over some of their summer earnings to purchase a trampoline…they have all flipped out! Marie attended volleyball camp in August.

Joanne, being thirteen, fervently defends her positions on whatever and does not like fakes or frills! She is easily satisfied as long as she finishes first! She has just accomplished her '93 goal of doing the splits.

We have no teenage flames or fixations to report at this time. Furthermore…

Vacation planned itself as Thomas attended the International Youth Rally in Estes Park. Two cousins his age also attended from Texas and California so the old people and younger clan hung out at a hostel facility. We forged up mountain trails, crossed fjords and frolicked in the sun. It was an experience exchanging conversation and food experiences with foreigners. We firmly recommend you do this!

In the midst of Midwest flooding came the yearly trek to Kansas City for the youth to have floating fellowship at 'Worlds of Fun' and take in a baseball game. What fate had Anya agree to be the other driver they needed? The rain was fierce. There were detours in addition to the already known detours. The trip was a fiasco with one frenzied driver! After a frantic day of errands Anya was ready to congratulate herself on perfect timing for a game at the high school when a girl failed to yield the right of way. Though no fault on her part, it was and still is a fuss! Thomas probably doesn't want me to mention his fender felony with Dad's Mercedes. He gave no flimsy excuses! But the children would want me to mention their $450 no frills Chevy sitting in the driveway just aching to be titled, licensed, insured, and driven to freedoms and fantasies only teenagers can fathom. Once again those who attest to being "fit as a fiddle", namely, Michael, Marie, Joanne and Anya, did the two mile walk/run Jingle Bell Run in Lincoln.

With four children bringing friends home we have become familiar with a lot of faces, among them the family of five boys of our missionary in Puerto Rico. We finally met him and his wife at the church women's convention while they were on furlough.

To start the year off right we returned four to school flushed with fever and flu!

And finally…

Still in our forties (alas, we have not found the 'fountain of youth')…slightly fatigued (nothing forty winks won't cure)… figures filled with extra flesh (so what's a little flab!)..Forever Friendly, Fat and Fred

P.S. Before you throw this in the furnace or yearn to point out flaws, just be glad I failed to delve into the atrocities of flatulence and fornication!

P.S.P.S. On the positive side: No fortune…no frozen assets!

The children were hard workers and obtained part time jobs. They were all able to get farm jobs with members. My idea was they could begin purchasing their own clothing and personal items. Not good enough for Frederick. As long as they had money they could contribute to high school tuition. However, there was no definite amount set so the children were always in limbo as to what amount of money they could call their own. Their decision to purchase a trampoline caused no small degree of tension. The cost per person was not extravagant but Frederick could not see past the total. Somehow the five young adults won out. The trampoline provided endless hours of enjoyment, especially with high school students brought home on the weekends.

And now it was time to think about driving lessons for the boys. Well, there was no way they would be allowed to touch the Mercedes and the large van was not a good learning vehicle. And the Lord steps in again. My mother wondered what to do for a Christmas present. A few hundred dollars bought an old car which all five used to learn how to drive and then were able to drive themselves back and forth to school.

Already when my children were in grade school I realized it would be up to me to teach the boys how to respect women and what the Bible teaches about husbands loving their wives within their God given leadership role. My daughters had to understand these traits needed to be present when it came time for them to choose a spouse. I often felt like I was walking a tightrope. I couldn't let them disrespect their father but at the same time they needed to know our relationship was not God-pleasing. I am convinced that mother's must play this role when their husbands refuse to raise their children with a loving example. It is most difficult. We mothers are the nurturers, the protectors. We feel our children's pain and at all costs want to keep them out of harm's way. We become even more like this if our children suffer from their father's uncontrolled anger. And so, if nurturing and protecting is all we do, we perpetuate marriages that engulf domestic violence. This is statistically proven. We cannot change our spouse's behavior. We must for the sake of our children and future generations take on the dual role inflicted on us. Leaving the sinful marriage, of course, is the other option.

Newsletter (Gazette) – 1994

High School Take Over

Besides holding some kind of record for having five children in high school at the same time…Frederick moved into the board chairman position. After serving as 2nd vice president and 1st vice president of the high school auxiliary, Anya moved up to the presidency.. What is everyone saying about this take over? If you hear please inform us!

And There Was Music

After academics and sports, fortunately there is still time for music! I think that makes the angels happy! Thomas was able to go on a Dakota tour last spring and enjoyed 'swing choir' competition. Michael also made tour choir this year. The rest belong to the general choirs…everyone belongs to band…Marie continues with piano.

Texas

The children's roots are bound in Texas so for a visit we did return. It was still a long way even though the boys (almost men) did most of the driving. It wasn't easy but we got Dad moving early in the morning and made it in one day. Had a wonderful time in a bay house with dear friends. Had several *Big* storms off the coast, caught a *Big* stingray, and ate *Big* shrimp at a former teacher's house.

Alpine, Wyoming

Well, it just seemed like a good idea. A chance to visit Anya's mother, Christmas being on Sunday meant only one Sunday service for Frederick to bow out of, and with children ready to leave the nest another memory together became an urgent must. Besides when did seven people ever agree on an activity? Now don't misunderstand – Dad didn't start out in full agreement. There was the money (but remember the present to do something special?!) and there was the weather (but just maybe there won't be a blizzard!) and so on. Well, the weather was perfect, no car problems, and best of all…seven people hit the slopes in Jackson and seven people returned none the worse for age or inexperience. 'Course they did have to stop the chairlift for a couple of us and Marie did have to be retrieved from over the cliff and the ski patrol did warn Thomas and Michael about their downhill speed. Meanwhile back in Anya's mother's and brother's apartment the food was always done to perfection. We had a beautiful honeymoon (?) suite compliments of Anya's mother and the snow covered mountains were breathtaking at every turn. We saw thousands of elk partaking in their winter feeds, bald eagles (Frederick could relate to them), mule deer and one wooden moose. Visited with Anya's younger brother and family on the way and on the way back through Rock Springs. And revisited old (as in have known for a long time) friends in Cheyenne.

Unemployment Statistics

Whatever they are they don't apply to us which makes me wonder how real they are. Even for under eighteen you can beat the regulations. Thomas worked two jobs because each one by law could only give him so many hours. Paul held onto his dishwashing/cooking job and still was able to work for farmers and a large detasseling company along with Michael. Marie at fifteen could only get so many hours at a local fast food restaurant but then had time for farm and detasseling jobs. Joanne was supposedly too young to hire but local farmers took her on and the detasseling company said they would give her a chance. She proved she was worthy of hire. Mom didn't even want a job but it was no problem filling in at the high school Thursday and Friday evenings cooking and serving supper. She has also doubled her time helping with catering. Even Dad could have had a second job at Schwann Enterprises but flat out declined! Thomas has switched to a Pizza Hut fifteen miles from the high school so he can work during the school year. Michael started at the Pizza Hut fifteen miles from home so he can work weekends and Paul is faithful to his restaurant on weekends. Marie was able to keep her fast food job on weekends and Joanne is able to work at school.

Lost Arts

It's so easy – when finished everyone wants a jar, yet they continue to deprive themselves of the fun. When cabbage hit an all time low of five cents a pound, we bought 235# and put up sauerkraut. Altogether thirteen people were involved – *Great Fun!* Second, but not so easy, would be making Springerle, a Christmas German tradition. Anya has decided to increase her time on this as many people are intrigued and pleased with receiving them. If you wish more information or would like to place an order…feel free to do so.

We always thought making bread would be a neat 'family thing' but alas it never materialized until Mom got a breadmaker machine for Christmas. And while it may not be the *family thing* we had in mind, the family definitely loves it and the bread machine is getting quite a work out.

Answering Machines Are Here To Stay

We have been among the minority trying to remain personable and not force people into talking to a machine, but we have relinquished our position for the sake of convenience. With all the children gone, Anya gone for two days, and Frederick in and out more and more, people are having trouble reaching us, so Dad was presented with his new toy for Christmas.

Health News

Dad now wears glasses but still has all his teeth. Mom is in process of acquiring bifocals has an occasional migraine, but still possesses all her faculties! Paul is on a three year allergy program. Michael and Marie were lucky enough to have our former dentist in Texas pull a tooth each to uncrowd their mouths.

Wanted

Parts for two dirt bikes.
Windshield and paint for '79 chevy four door.

Sports Update

Even though some are out for every sport offered at the high school no one has won any great awards or single handedly carried their team to victory. But conditioning is another matter. Some statistics: Benching; Thomas-230…Michael-210…Paul-200…Marie-90…Joanne-85…Dad-150…Mom-able to sit for long periods. Squatting; Thomas-400…Michael-300…Paul-280…Marie?…Joanne?…Dad-bad knee…Mom-able to get down but not back up.

Crimestoppers

Please call if you have any information which could lead to the arrest of individual entering garage door somewhere between the hours of 2am and 5am on Saturday evenings. This is the third Mercedes emblem stolen.

Used Cars

1978 Mercedes…works most of the time, $2500 or best offer…Diesel…does not start in winter…cord for plug-in extra!

1984 Chevy van…lots of miles, works most of time, $3000 or best offer… Diesel… does not start in winter…cord for plug-in extra.

Snacks To The Max Closed

Entrepreneurs, faithful patrons of Sams, having reached their full potential in providing "goodies" for the high school students were officially closed at the beginning of the '94-'95 school year. The reason in writing was "lack of closet space". Or was it too much competition with the school canteen???

College Room Needed

Depending acceptance and financial feasibility, Thomas may need lodging near Yale, Rice, Carnegie Melon, or Northwestern. If you know of anything please contact as soon as possible.

My children were fairly decent at remembering my birthday and Mother's Day, but being away at school, sometimes they forgot. When they realized their forgetfulness they told me there was a large present in the future. This actually became kind of a joke, this large present growing in size over a couple of years. Well, I had always wanted a fountain. I did purchase a cheap plastic one but it did not make it through the winter. Once, on a bridge excursion to a small town, I discovered a huge family owned business that made fountains...beautiful fountains. I told the children about it. Finally, two of them went with me to pick one out. We went from room to room, the fountains growing in size and becoming more ornate with each room we entered. When we were in the room with the largest fountains they were ready to make a purchase. I insisted this was not necessary and we should move backwards to another room. They would not listen to me. And so a three tier fountain with two lovebirds atop was chosen and purchased. It was disassembled to fit into our van and we headed home. I anticipated a loud and negative reaction from Frederick. The children decided to start by just bringing in one piece at a time so as not to overwhelm their father. It didn't work. They had scattered the pieces in different areas but by the time he saw them all his reaction was of volcanic proportions. The amount of money spent was ridiculous...explaining it came from five children to cover events for at least two years did not help. What would the members of the church think to see such an extravagant display in our front yard? And so the pieces lay separated. The next day a friend stopped over and was shown the pieces and learned of Frederick's unwillingness to have them put together. She was shocked. Soon others learned of the unassembled gift. A week later Frederick was absent, attending a conference. Two families we were closest to came over with farming equipment and cement. A place on the side of the house was chosen and the area was prepared for the fountain. It was assembled and hooked up to water. It was awesome. Boy was I scared but at least I had these two very strong families behind me. We had begun to grill for supper and Frederick showed up. What could he say? And so, I had my fountain. While this was an aggressive move, concession was made in not putting the fountain in the front yard where it begged to be.

Meanwhile I attended as many of the children's functions as possible. Frederick resented my trips and the gas it cost. Speaking of gas, I stopped to fill up the van once on the way to the high school. Whoops! I was putting regular gas in instead of diesel. Some children were with me. They said if I started it, it would blow up, ha,ha. I was immediately apprehensive of Frederick's wrath and could not think clearly. But the gas was drained, diesel put in and we were on our way…the children sworn to secrecy.

One of Frederick's school board meetings coincided with a volleyball game night. Marie noticed her dad sitting in the bleachers and at half time went over to say hi. She wondered why he was there and asked if he had a meeting. Enough said! Frederick did, however, have time to attend school events of member's children. His children knew this and I know it hurt them especially when he related to them how talented some of these member's children were. We were all to understand and accept that this was part of his ministry.

On our trip to Wyoming we first stopped at my brother and family's house. The nine cousins had a great reunion. On the morning to leave Frederick told Thomas and Michael to load up the van. They balked. Again I do not understand this forthright disobedience. It was their turn to be slapped. The van was packed and we left. Frederick was very angry. He stopped at Wal-Mart and asked me to speak to my sons while he was in the store. I told them I was sorry for the slapping but said the right thing as far as them being disobedient

Newsletter - 1995

Places To Go: Colorado…Thomas and Michael spent time with friends and were able to ski. Illinois…Obviously Dad's love for the White Sox influenced Thomas to attend this university and possibly the fact that they accepted him. What an experience to get around in Chicago and spend the night on the fourteenth floor over-looking the city. Thomas's dorm is off campus overlooking Lake Michigan. He has no social life. He studies, works, and has found a ride to church. He seems content and the phone bill shows he has not forgotten where he came from. Nebraska…an estimate of trips to the high school shows the Chevy ahead with 72, next the van with 30 and the Mercedes last with 20 trips.

Texas…Frederick visited his personal auto dealer to 'upgrade' the Mercedes. Thomas and Michael were able to visit old acquaintances on choir tour. Wisconsin…Frederick attended a Principal's conference and Marie was there for the annual choral festival. Frederick made a quick trip back in June to visit his mother.

People To See: Cousin Michael and family graced our doorstep on their way to Texas. Our dear nanny stopped in and became Thomas's personal senior picture photographer. Our synod president stops at the high school on occasion to visit his daughter which makes us all feel very proud and special. A dear old acquaintance from California days was privileged to buy us a cup of expensive coffee at the St. Louis airport. We pray for his wife who is fighting leukemia. Governor Ben Nelson attended a business anniversary celebration which Anya happened to be helping cater. Served him tea, shook his hand, and has a picture to prove it. Anya's brother and family found Nebraska after four and a half years (talk about lost). We were given thirty hours notice on December 24th, that they would be coming. Anya's mother came for Thomas's graduation festivities. Our missionary friends from Puerto Rico came for their son's graduation (Thomas's best friend) so we celebrated together. The ten males from the two families sang for church Sunday…*Rise Up O Men of God*…it was glorious!! Their son stayed for the summer. Two more sons came mid-July. Doctors…The February/March virus was not friendly! Michael and Paul started with bronchitis, were reinfected taking Marie and Joanne down with then the second time. Paul and Joanne ended up in the emergency room with streptococcus and bilateral otitis media (extra charge for big words and Sunday). Finally Thomas went along with the bronchitis. But Frederick carried this to the max! He was SO sick he went to the doctor where he received drugs for all kinds of unmentionable things. Knowing full well his body doesn't like artificial chemicals, he still followed the doctor's orders...which led to fainting, a fractured rib, blurred eye sight, temporary loss of vision, and headaches. A cat scan showed nothing. Went off the medicine and recovered. Sports and related injuries: Thomas suffered months of chondromalacia from football; Michael with weeks of swollen ankle syndrome, also from football; Paul with a splinted finger for six weeks for tendon damage from football and from wrestling prolonged water on the elbow; Michael again with six weeks splinted finger for tendon damage from wrestling; Marie would like mention of her thumb from volleyball; Anya...usual five or so sinus infections but there is hope on the horizon.

Things To Do:
Cemetery...Put in bid to mow twenty acre cemetery and get it! Buy 'Dixon' lawn mower and hire friends to mow and weed-eat for a total of one hundred man hours...repeat every two weeks. Honor Roll...Be overachievers! All five managed to maintain honor roll status. We are proud of them! Iron Man... Paul achieved this for the second year during football camp. Michael was second. Tour choir...Marie joins. Manager...Anya volunteered some summer time to meet with the high school administrator and discuss reorganizing the kitchen. Little did she know she would end up with a job. She keeps temporary in front so everyone knows the job is open. Co-manager started two days before school and started off with a fire on the stove. Money...leave some behind when you move and then it will be so exciting when a friend calls and says your name is listed in the paper to collect money before it is turned over to the state. Motorcycle...let your kids have broken ones so they spend most of their time working on them. Let friend's children use them so you can spend the first evening of their arrival in the emergency room getting to know them. Owls...offer to help cook for an OWLS (organization of senior Lutherans) retreat and end up doing the whole thing. Videos should be purchased for exercising and developing six packs. Weight...lifting equipment should also be purchased and if necessary kept upstairs in the bedroom. This is more important than beds.

And through it all;

Sing praises to God, sing praises!
Sing praises to our King, sing praises!
For God is the king of all the earth;
Sing praises with a psalm!

Ps. 47

One day I noticed an ad in the paper for bids on mowing the cemetery. The boys were excited. Frederick said it was a stupid idea beyond their capabilities. We won! Thomas figured out costs etc. They made a bid and had one of the highest paying jobs imaginable for children their age. When pressed for time they simply hired other boys from their high school.

Joanne was next to come under her Father's wrath. We were all sitting in the living room. I do not remember the discussion but all of a sudden Frederick flew across the room and started slapping his youngest daughter. She made haste to leave when he was finished. As the youngest, she was grossly embarrassed for this happening in front of her older siblings. She was more sensitive anyway. And once more, the amazing thing is, she does not remember this incident.

And then came a dark day. One evening I went upstairs to watch television. I could not open the door. After some commotion Frederick opened the door. He mumbled something and then took a tape out of the video player and left. The next day at supper time Frederick was missing. His study was in the house and the vehicles were not gone so where was he? He finally showed up and mumbled about doing something at church. My gut was telling me there was something not right. That night he was watching television again and came down to bed later than usual. What was going on? The next morning after he left to teach his religion class at school I went into his study. I began looking around not really knowing what I was searching for. I found the video in back of the bottom drawer of his desk. I took it upstairs and popped it in. Wow! I started sweating and became nauseated. It wasn't hard core pornography (as he would later tell the counselor) but there it was…*nudity*! I did not remember where I started it so I replaced it in the drawer with a note saying I was sorry I had lost his place. Frederick returned from school. Soon he came out of the study

77

angrier than all get out. How dare I leave a note instead of confronting him...
what?! He raved on! I finally responded with "damn it, how dare you turn
this on me and make it my fault" (first time I ever swore in front of him).
Now he was so irate I knew he was seconds away from slapping me. I kept
my distance! Luckily he was under a time constraint to leave for an area
conference. As he was preparing for departure I asked if he could promise
me he would never do this again. His answer, "You know it is wrong to
promise in uncertain things." He left. I paced like a crazy person. I believe
this is the only time I had a drink before noon, a martini at that. I called
our former district president. I have no idea why I chose to talk with him.
When he came to the phone I related the incident in Texas, when the pastors
were laughing that by process of elimination, Frederick must statistically be
the wife abuser. He was silent. I then told him about the pornography tape
I found and Frederick's response. He responded that certainly in marriage
promises should be made otherwise he had no suggestions but gave me the
church's 800 help line number. I was able to get hold of Frederick that night
and insisted that in marriage one should be able to promise there would be
no more disobedience of the sixth commandment. Did he agree? Hard to
say. There was a lot of stammering without actually agreeing or disagreeing.
Two weeks later I answered the phone (Frederick answered right after me).
It was a video store thirty miles away asking about two videos that were
due. The strangest conversation then took place between the lady calling
and Frederick. I finally took it for a stammering attempt to cover up the title
"Obsession"! So much for the sixth commandment and a promise to correct
this marriage destroying weakness.

During the summer Frederick announced his plans to go visit his mother.
No big deal except there had not been any family outings for some time and
there were no future plans for family or just the two of us. Nothing unusual
there. So I voiced this. Never a good idea! He became irate and covered all
of my problems finally ending with a diagnosis. I was a borderline alcoholic
with a personality disorder and a tendency toward manic depression! Wow!!
As he yelled I lowered my head for protection against physical contact and
edged my way out of the kitchen towards the laundry room and back door.
I made it out the back door (still in my bathrobe), down the stairs and stood
on the lawn a safe distance from him. Having space between us I dared to
speak back to him. He suggested I just get out..."why don't you just leave?"

Hmmm, what a great idea. I had honestly never considered it. I waited in the backyard for awhile so his anger would subside then went inside, found some clothes in the laundry room, dressed, and walked up the hill to our dear friend's house. They were shocked to hear not just at what had taken place but that these encounters had been going on our entire married life. However, they were not shocked at Frederick's lack of interest in his wife and family. I was the one who was surprised that this was obvious to them. So much for thinking you are hiding the dirty laundry. Now I was emotionally concerned for my daughters who were home and suppose to be leaving soon for work. Would Frederick use them now for his verbal venting? Would he not give them a ride to work? Mr. friend went down to the parsonage, talked to Frederick and then gave the girls a ride to work. Meanwhile I called the 800 number. I was already harboring guilt for thinking I might not return immediately. As I relayed this guilt to the phone counselor he asked if my presence with Frederick enabled him to act out against the fifth commandment. The answer was of course yes. Then maybe it would be better if I stayed away and sought counseling. The counselor also asked me if I understood that Frederick's acting out was due to low self-esteem. Now there was an epiphany. I always assumed he had an inflated ego. Mr. friend called the elders of the congregation and later that evening there was a meeting where I finally disclosed to outsiders the truths of our codependent abusive relationship. They quickly decided the district president had to be involved. I met with him the next day. I had never hit it off with this pastor and so was surprised at his empathy.

I was not comfortable staying up the hill with my friends so I moved into a motel fifteen miles away. Frederick called; I should come home and what was I thinking putting the cost of a motel on the credit card. I worried about my daughters being with Frederick as he might vent his rage on them. And sure enough he told them it was partly their fault for not keeping their room cleaned and helping out in the house. He was obsessed with their room, which true it was in disarray, but they were gone to school and worked so much of the time it never seemed that big of a deal. I told them to spend time at our friends up the hill if they needed to get away. The year before, I had taken over managing the high school kitchen. During this summer I spent time preparing for the new school year. My next trip to the high school brought me in contact with the school administrator who was actually a friend of Frederick. Because of this I hesitated to say too much about my husband. But into the conversation he asked if there was ever any physical abuse. Of course he was visibly disturbed at my answer. He did give me permission to move into the girl's dormitory for the summer if necessary.

Frederick found a counselor. At our first meeting Frederick narrowed in on the girl's room. I mean he went on and on about this while the counselor and I just looked at each other. Even I had never seen him in this state of unrelated obsession. The counselor finally asked me how I viewed this. In the whole scope of our marital problems, I stated, it seemed low on the list and he readily agreed. I had a meeting alone with the counselor the next day. He was forthright. Did I have access to funds? I should avail myself of some. I was shocked. Ending the marriage had not entered my mind. He then explained to me that there was very little chance of Frederick admitting his guilt much less changing. People his age were established in their defense mechanisms. Ministers were the hardest of all to crack. I was dumbfounded. I did not meet with him again! A couple of days later, still at the motel, I received a surprising call from the high school secretary whom I had come to know fairly well. Another reminder that all is not necessarily as we perceive. The secretary and her husband had major marital issues many years back and partook of counseling for some time while living apart. To this end she called to give me the name of their Christian counselor. They had been to several before they found this one whom they were both comfortable with and respected. We did make an appointment and did see him and he was marvelous. We were told separation was a must at this point. Our first assignment…a date! Frederick did call and we did go out for an afternoon and it was ok. Several meetings later I brought up the pornography tape. Frederick responded that it was not really pornography. The counselor pushed that it was indeed nudity and therefore pornography. Frederick somewhat agreed but certainly didn't come across that he considered it that big of a deal. When pressed on the issue he offered the information that he had been doing this for ten years. Another shocker!! Why in fact did he choose ten years? Smoking was brought up. The counselor suggested I was an adult and this was my decision. Funny, that is what my grade school girls had insinuated on a visit to Frederick's mother. How could their father forbid me, another adult, not to smoke? From the mouths of babes! Well, he could, because out of fear, I let him. Codependency!

The counselor was able to meet with all five children in one session. They all presented the same scenarios. Marie offered that she had seen her father slap me...no way! She was not born yet. But the fighting she heard must have carried her to that step as if it was real.

I had been planning on attending Women's Missionary conference. So the next week I moved to a friend's house who would also be attending the conference. What a wonderful spiritual break. Oh it was awkward at times when asked about Frederick. The greatest was meeting a second cousin and his wife whom I hung out with as much as possible. His similarities to my father, now eleven years dead, were remarkable.

Back home, the district president set up counseling for Frederick and me at the church body home base in Wisconsin. I was picked up from the airport by a pastor, a mutual friend of ours. He took me to rent a car. Oh horrors! I was totally out of my comfort zone, which was very small, having spent most of my married life at home. At their home for supper, the story had to be told albeit I did not declare all of the abuse. Amazing that everyone is so shocked when abuse is so rampant even among Christians. I was put up in a Holiday Inn. Frederick stayed elsewhere. We met the following day, Thursday. I assumed this counselor had been filled in on our marital discord so was surprised he didn't take more of a lead but rather wanted to know what we hoped to get out of the counseling. Therefore, not much was brought to light. He would see us the next day, Friday, and then not until Monday. Afternoon and evening were soooooo long by myself, not knowing anyone, not confident to drive anywhere. Next day I was totally an emotional basket case especially knowing I had the weekend alone ahead of me. I arrived early for our counseling session in order to speak to the counselor alone before Frederick arrived. The counselor, admitting he had not been told anything at all about our marital problems, said he would meet with Frederick first and then me. I wandered through the office complex, near tears, sometimes giving in to crying. Finally I was with the counselor and poured out my heart. He looked into my eyes and told me straightforward I had to calm down and just repeat the facts to make myself believable and not give in to hysteria. I informed him I was going home. He understood and said it was most important at this time that I was with a support group. I was soon on a plane headed home. With Frederick gone I was able to stay at our home a few days. As I sat out on the porch one afternoon I had a visitor, a female member from our church, whom I knew better than some. The congregation talking and taking sides had occurred to me and I figured Frederick, who was well liked, came out far ahead of me with my frequent wit, sometimes on the cutting edge. Of 200 members, just this one lady came to me, not to judge, not to find out the gory details, but to offer her support and at least get the facts straight to ward off any malicious gossip. I was glad to have this meeting before the opposite came to me via a letter the next week. The letter, from a female church member, judged me, chewed me up one side and down the other, leaving me to shake like a leaf in a wind storm.

I needed a place to stay before Frederick returned. I called the principal of the high school to confirm his offer for staying in the dormitory. That way I could also do my job as kitchen manager. I soon found out Frederick was a very busy person on the phone with *my* support group. The first was a good friend from Texas. She sounded suspiciously different, guarded responses, definitely not usual for her. Soon she sought to *counsel* me??? Maybe it wasn't so bad, maybe I wasn't thinking clearly, maybe it would be better if I returned home. She used phrases similar to Frederick's diagnosis for me, borderline alcoholic with a personality disorder and a tendency toward manic depression. What was this all about? Finally it came to the surface that she had had a long conversation with Frederick. I was devastated, uttering with disbelief that she would buy into his story. I quietly signed off and hung up. I needed my mother, not a usual need for me, and called. Oh my goodness! Now you must understand that my mother is easily swayed. Anyway, I tried to remember this while absorbing the similar story I had heard from my turncoat friend in Texas. Of course I could talk my mother back to the reality of the situation and the hard fact of Frederick's ability to manipulate. He called my mother... *my* mother! Did this man have no shame? Now I was passed distraught. I was angry! I made one more call; my sister-in-law. Yes, Frederick had called her too but I'm sure regretted it. Delilah does not go peacefully into the night. Frederick, I'm sure barely got two sentences out before receiving an earful and a large dose of reality. I don't believe they have spoken since.

> When the righteous cry for help, the Lord hears, and delivers them out of all their troubles. The Lord is near to the brokenhearted, and saves the crushed in spirit.

> Psalm 34:17-18

Frederick and I continued to meet with the local counselor recommended by the secretary. We made slow progress. The counselor did not recommend living together. Five problem areas were identified; emotional abuse, control, affection, communication, and marriage versus ministry as to time and energy. As hard as it was for Frederick to accept emotional abuse, it was a long needed reality check for me. Emotional abuse includes raising voice, standing, arms in motion, lengthy orations, commands, inflicting guilt, demeaning the person, and being uncompassionate. Wow, that was our marriage in a nutshell. Control involves emotional abuse, regulating time, demanding jobs and regulating money. Affection should include both physical and verbal love communication. There should be eye contact while showing empathy and interest. There should be active listening as an equal and there should be civility. Frederick was counseled to validate my feelings and not minimize past hurts. We were advised to set goals for the future. I was to be involved with all planning. I was to set boundaries on Frederick's behaviors. I needed to replace the anger and resentment which fueled my existence with cultivating a marital relationship. Expressing the love of God to each other had to be part of this relationship. He suggested books to read. Frederick chose to read books from our church body's book store, underlining sections applicable to my inadequacies in the marriage relationship, and then giving me the book to read. He loved one book, describing what a sexual man is, almost giving the go ahead to act out on lustful desires. It was evident during our counseling sessions that Frederick's goals were to prove I had no reason to leave him and that I did not correctly perceive the problems in our marriage.

Where was I to stay after school started? Once again the school secretary came through. She suggested I go to a town just ten miles from the school. There was a senior apartment complex and perhaps the owner would make an exception for me. She did! Thank-you Lord! This was too funny. My parents actually lived there when I was born though the hospital was in another town. My full circle of life complete, or so I thought. Little did I know there would still be many miles to go on my earthly journey. I had nothing to furnish this apartment. I bought one glass, one cup and some paper supplies. I called my eldest son and asked him to bring me a few items. He brought enough to make me comfortable including a living room chair. When I asked why he bothered he said because it was my devotion chair.

Ah, we do make an impact on our children. And so I did my kitchen job at the high school and had counseling sessions once a week.

Eventually I moved back home. I remember an evening outside, Frederick and I talking, when I lit up a cigarette. He was shocked but controlled himself admirably and joked about my new independence.

Then there was the meeting with officers and elders from both churches and the three pastors of the praesidium. I was asked to attend. If you are not a member of a conservative church body you cannot appreciate how unorthodox it was for this to happen. It soon became apparent that the district president had an agenda and that was to get rid of Frederick. He dragged our marital problems into Frederick's ministry, drawing unsubstantiated comparisons. I was shocked. Frederick was livid. Where was this guy coming from? I had specifically and emphatically stated the first time I met with him that Frederick's relationships with his family were totally isolated from any relationships outside the family. I restated this in front of this room of men. Eventually, the president from the smaller church said his peace, got up to leave, and resigned his office as president. The larger church tended to side with the district president.

Next was a meeting with the district president. A couple, members of the small church, requested they be allowed to attend. This was in fact the lady I had received the scathing letter of denouncement from when I first separated. The meeting was a joke. The district president began by informing us he had talked to our former district president. Then he hung his head and began a most dramatic thought process. He came up for air to say he was trying to find the words to best describe what he meant to convey. His head went back down and nodded from left to right as he wrestled with the words he should use. Finally, he declared he could think of no other way than just to spit it out. While our relationships within the congregation at our previous church were basically good, I had on several occasions become at odds with members "because of my big mouth." Wow! This man had four years of college and four years in the seminary, language being a very important tool of the trade, and this was all the better he could do? But this moment took on a heart warming glow, one of the best in our marriage, as Frederick took the stand to defend me. He pronounced my ability to connect with people. In fact whenever we left a church it was I who maintained friendships. When the occasion presented itself for us to return for a visit Frederick stated they were genuinely more enamored to see me than him. And so I thank this pastor for his crudeness and insulting words to give Frederick a chance to lovingly speak out for me. Later, I wondered if he was just saying the right thing in front of his members. I have no idea what game this pastor was playing. First he empathizes with me...then he turns what I say in confidence to run Frederick's ministry into the ground in front of parishioners...then he viciously turns on me... perhaps because I spoke up for Frederick.

The next day the district president gave Frederick an option: either resign and the president would see that he was put on a call list or if Frederick did not resign, he would give him a year's leave of absence with counseling. This was so totally not protocol. The blessing of all this was for a short time Frederick and I were united against the mutual enemy. Frederick of course could not imagine a year off with counseling and so resigned. This unfavorable outcome made me the villain for putting his ministry in jeopardy. I was emphatically told to think twice before I ever engaged in such folly again. Sadly, he was not confronted personally about his abuse and sexual immorality. "Brethren, if a man is overtaken in any trespass, you who are spiritual should restore him in a spirit of gentleness. Look to yourself, lest you too be tempted. Bear one another's burdens, and so fulfill the law of Christ. (Galations:1-2)

ARKANSAS
Is there a choice?

Newsletter (Gazette) - 1996

Church has received word that Frederick has accepted their call. The church is ninety plus souls. His ministry will also include a temporary vacancy to a church one hundred miles to the southeast. This followed Frederick's resignation from the two congregations in Nebraska. This was a result of the pressure from the district praesidium "for the good of the ministry". Neither the average life span, this column, or this author's day afford enough time to go into all the details concerning that. It is indeed comforting to know that God is in charge of our lives, not men! The aforementioned followed a leave of absence for us to recharge our marriage and strengthen our communication skills which we did through reading and the aid of a very wonderful Christian counselor. We are happy to share our acquired knowledge with anyone and recommend to anyone needing an overhaul to do it now! We thank everyone for their prayers and support.

Frederick's mother is sadly suffering from Alzheimer's but still resides at home. Frederick found time to visit her twice. The last half of December was spent setting up an office at the church, a first for Frederick, and trying to find an empty space for a nap between boxes, wife, and five children arriving home.

Anya bravely had her maxillary sinuses cleaned out and a small bone piece collecting bacteria removed. As you read this it will have been one year without a sinus infection. Frederick provided nursing care for a week. Before leaving Nebraska, Anya used her massage gift...a first, and found it to be the closest thing to heaven on this earth. The greatest tribute of the year was a fountain presented by all five children on Mother's Day. Not only was Anya able to attend the women's convention in Green Bay but met a second cousin and his dear wife. With the move to Arkansas Anya had to leave her job as cafeteria manager at the high school. Anya took the long way to Arkansas through Milwaukee and Chicago; in fact, with the return trip to Nebraska for the girl's Christmas concert she hit eight states in ten days. Anya's mother was able to visit in May.

Thomas...took over the mowing business for the summer. He bought a 'kitchen' in September and headed for Chicago in the Chevy Impala. He and three roommates decided to save money by cooking their own meals which mostly Thomas did. The Impala, locked in the parking lot, was stolen by two teenagers followed later by a high speed chase and ending in the side of a brick house. Trial is pending. Thomas is not returning to the University of Chicago. He is going to put a new twist on homeschooling outlining his own courses. However, he may take a couple classes at the Arkansas university because it is cheaper than buying his own health insurance. He will earn room and board by cooking unpronounceable dishes for Mom and helping Dad on the computer.

Michael and Paul...graduated from high school on a Saturday afternoon in May. On Sunday an open house was held for them while they packed. Monday they left for Marine boot camp in San Diego. Michael overtook Paul the last week and was #1 physically fit in his platoon. They were home for a week and then back to Camp Pendleton. After two weeks they flew to Missouri to complete their reserve training in engineering. Paul finished top of his class, with Michael a very close third. Paul is now a lance corporal and Michael is a private, 1st class. They will both be attending a Lutheran College in Wisconsin this semester and will spend one weekend a month in Green Bay for drills. Marie and Joanne...are still attending high school in Nebraska. They played volleyball (Joanne was captain), sang in the tour choir, were active in student council and danced on the spirit squad. Marie was homecoming queen. Joanne also plays basketball and is presently high scorer. *Snowstorm*! It hit in March. Michael was ten miles from the high school and could not get back. He stayed overnight with the Pizza Hut manager. Marie was with the tour choir stranded in Nebraska City at Subway. Paul and Joanne crawled the last five miles to the high school turnoff from the interstate and had to spend the night in a restaurant. They had much company and Joanne played bridge with a school superintendent.

God bless you all throughout 1997. What a wonderful thing to have Christian friends and relatives all over the earth. The "heavenly feast" will truly be great!

Early in the summer I made mention of attending Michael and Paul's graduation from boot camp. I was already looking forward to it and just assumed we would attend. Frederick said that was ridiculous. How many parents would travel across the country for this? I thought everyone would. He said that was not going to happen. This came up during our counseling. The counselor thought it was very reasonable but said it would be a mistake at this time for us to travel together. Well, since the counselor thought the trip for this event was reasonable, Frederick changed his tune and decided to go. However, none of the children wanted to ride with him so he gave it up. We had a splendid trip. Yes, all the parents were there. Michael and Paul were disappointed their father did not come. The trip home was updating them on the condition of our marriage.

Three situations happened that gave me hope, false hope that is. There had finally been some counseling and the children were for the most part on their own. I thought money would not be as much of an issue...*Wrong*! I thought without the children we would spend more time together...*Wrong*! I thought there would be more understanding after counseling...*Wrong*! Once established in Arkansas, life deteriorated to what it had been before. The marriage resumed the same old patterns. Lunch and dinner on time were top priorities. I should always be available to help fold any church related materials and volunteer for any church position no one else wanted to do. He did what he wanted and bought what he wanted. The same restrictions on my spending and time outside the home were in place coupled with resentment, sarcasm, anger, or just ignoring me. The only outside activity he wanted to see from me was making money. I did earn some money for a while. One of our members opened a restaurant and hired me. It was hard work but it was a great crew to work with. It offered another benefit. Frederick was willing to eat there to support this member.

My beautiful fountain stood in our front yard. One day a couple came to the front door inquiring where I had obtained it...too funny...this very fountain which had ignited a vesuvian response from Frederick iniated a friendship with these two complete strangers. They took instructions from Frederick and became members of our church. They welcomed our family over for get-togethers whenever the children were home. After all the forgotten birthdays and all the birthday parties I gave for Frederick, I finally decided not to be disappointed and came right out and asked for a party for my fiftieth birthday. I truly do not believe he would ever have been able to put something together if it had not been for our fountain friend. She had to lead him by the nose and did more than half the work herself. It is so often a fine line between unwilling to show love and just not having a clue how to go about it. I actually felt sorry for him except that he thoroughly enjoyed the time and attention from our attractive fountain friend.

With the children gone from home I began to enjoy decorating and finding good deals at garage sales to enhance the ambience of our home. A couple children tilled an area for me so I could finally have the herb garden I had always dreamed of having. Frederick hated this because he would have to mow around it.

Newsletter - 1997

Accident just when life seemed to be coming together. The policeman said Thomas was following too close but he has measurements and pictures to show the impossibility of this. However his insurance adjuster isn't interested and he can't get a court hearing because no ticket was issued. Oh yes, the other driver was a wealthy, well known citizen.

Bridge offered new opportunities in the form of duplicate for ACBL (American contract bridge league) master points. Frederick declined to be Anya's partner in these 'stressful' situations so it became a mother-son bimonthly endeavor. The payoffs were several 1st and 2nd places and also a regional lower division win in Little Rock. Anya has a new partner since Thomas forsook her. Anya hopes to tryout in Tunisia some year for international games. Bridge headquarters by the way are in Memphis.

Colorado keeps popping up in our lives. Joanne has particular interest in Boulder, home of her boyfriend. Thomas and Michael grabbed a few skiing days. Marie and Joanne were there for choir tour ending up snow bound in Casper, Wyoming. Marie joined a group in June for camping and rafting.

Daring stunts would include Michael sky diving and Marie swimming across the Arkansas River (details much too involved for this letter...watch for paperback edition). Thomas tried flying while rock climbing. Their guardian angels get very little rest!

Employment has not been a problem yet. Marie had a cooking and waitressing job, Joanne also waitressing and working for Mom. Michael and Paul landed several jobs through a job service managed by one of our members. Thomas went from part-time to full-time for the manager of the same job service. Thomas now sells computers and tutors people as a Hand Technologies Consultant. Frederick is quite busy with his two churches and Anya continues to work on her grade school spelling series.

Friends from Memphis drove over for Champagne on the 'mount' and a six year catch-up since Texas days. Our neighbors from Nebraska said life was too quiet and came for bridge and fellowship on the mount. Boys had a group from Nebraska visit in July. Marie brought a group home before graduation.

Graduation..Marie's turn. We joined friends in Nebraska to celebrate and started all over with 'Open House' when we got home. Marie attended local university staying at home with her old-fashioned parents. She also took up interior decorating in her room.

Heaven…Frederick's mother awaits our Lord's return following a fall, broken hip, surgery and infections. Michael and Paul were able to attend the funeral with their father. Another dear friend, from Cheyenne days, also left this vale of tears after a hard-fought battle against cancer.

Investments..Frederick, we told you to stay in Wal-Mart!

Illness..very little. Only one sinus infection for Anya since her surgery and only one broken toe.

Jamaica was visited by Michael for ten days over Christmas vacation for a special biology credit.

Knights at the high school,Marie and Joanne played soccer, and Joanne, volleyball and basketball...also both sang in the choir.

Longview, Texas is where Thomas now lives. The more he got involved at home with church, work, cooking, and computer help the less he studied. So he decided it was time to get out, make money, and get back to studying. He is now a member and the newly-elected treasurer of Lone Star Lutheran in Tyler. He occasionally plays the organ.

Milwaukee is where Michael and Paul attend college. Marie will be joining them. They are doing very well and are not afraid to engage teachers in critical and thoughtful theological discussions.

The brothers three, met to go through their mother's house. Anya and her sister-in-law joined them after attending the women's convention in Duluth and visiting family and friends in Eau Claire. A lot of work sorting, cleaning, and dividing.

Organ players in our new church consisted of one. Thomas, being younger and more talented, was given the first opportunity. He installed the new hymnal organ software. After he left desperation put Anya next on the list. So bifocals, new hymnal, et all excuses did not work and she is back on the bench.

Peaches, "yes, children, pick as many as you like." Anya regretted those words and still there were more to can, freeze and make jam from.

Queen Marie was asked to appear in Nebraska in October to crown the new queen. The *queen mother* accompanied her and had tears when the new queen turned out to be Joanne.

Conway was easy enough to learn. By the time Frederick called on the members he even knew the surrounding areas. The children love the ease of getting to outside recreational sites. Marie is getting to know the policemen as they eat free at Shoney's where she cooks…Not! It's more one on one encounters. Paul and Joanne even have pictures of one such encounter in front of our house.

Summer brought everyone together again. Luckily some were usually gone to work or play otherwise we would surely have fallen over each other. Frederick had his study to retreat to and Anya knew August and an empty house would come soon enough! Love it when the children are home and we are able to sing together in church.

Texas also is back in our lives. Frederick attended four conferences during the year. Thanksgiving was celebrated with Joanne, her boyfriend, and Marie. The Sunday after, Frederick and Anya drove down to Longview to see how Thomas was fending in his first apartment.

United States Marine Corps has promoted Michael to Lance Corporal and Paul to Corporal. They still put in their once-a-month weekend in Green Bay and had their two week drill this May in California. They sent home boxes of unused MREs (meals ready to eat).

Vienna Boys Choir performed at Wisconsin Lutheran College in Milwaukee. Anya had hoped to join Michael and Paul but the trip seemed too much.

Another trip to Nebraska to bring Joanne home for Christmas. Anya and Marie and two members on the way up to Nebraska and added Michael, Paul, and Joanne for the return. Wyoming was awesome in September when Anya visited her mother. Hiking, bridge, and sightseeing were relaxing. Anya's brother amicably did his part hosting. Riding on the back of a four-wheeler up a mountain was a thrill, courtesy of one of mother's friends.

Xmas is always special as we reflect on God sending his perfect son down to this miserable earth to save all its inhabitants. My favorite gift request was from Paul..Pieper's Christian Dogmatics.

Yellow was no where to be seen in the new house so Anya had to so some painting and wallpapering. Frederick helped to do some paneling.

Zealous we must all be to carry out God's great command. Encourage each other and pray for each other. Love to all

Frederick never asked my opinion on financial matters so I was very surprised when he asked about stock investments. I immediately stated Wal-Mart would be my choice. He invested and shortly after shifted this investment to another company his broker recommended. I never let him forget it as stocks in Wal-Mart went off the charts.

The year after we moved to Arkansas Thomas quit college at the University of Chicago. He felt they charged an unreasonable amount of money for extracurricular opportunities that he did not take advantage of and felt he could just as easily learn on his own (which he had the drive to do) free of charge. Major upset with his father who could comprehend only

One path in life: college, job, marry, home. Thomas stayed with us for seven months. In lieu of rent he helped around the house, cooked etc. It was during this stay I found out how much money Thomas had invested in college. I asked him why he never asked for help. He took my high school graduation letter very seriously when I said being independent also demanded some financial independence. I tried to rectify this with Frederick but it was too late now that Thomas had quit. Thomas finally was able to purchase a used vehicle and left for Texas hoping to start his own computer business. Frederick would not help him financially because he quit college. My son did as well as he could on his own staying in a run-down dirty apartment. I visited him on several occasions and we enjoyed playing bridge together. Without capital for advertising he finally gave up his idea.

When the children were home during parts of the summer Frederick always pushed them to be helping him and doing outside jobs for him. They had jobs and were not opposed to helping but he became obsessed with controlling their time and getting everything possible out of them while they were home. And there was the arguing. Since he had never established instructional communication with them every subject became heated. They were most upset when he used very important pastors who got all 'As' in school as resources and authorities on religious matters, rather than using proofs from the Bible. They were always glad to leave.

Newsletter (Chronicle) - 1998

The coast to coast caravanning ceased long enough to bring us together for three days and a family picture. The conception this year as is characteristic in these continuous noncontroversial correspondences is…well, I concede to your cranial capacity to reach this conclusion on your own. Communicating with four-and-a-half college students challenges the most competent and confident parent…consequently those of us in a chronological crisis are hurting! Our thoughts, words and actions have been collectively critiqued! The statements this year are factual being presented in the first person and therefore not contingent on interpretation or misrepresentation.

MARIE: (Editor's note: Marie chooses non conformity by eliminating the letter "C".) Though I would like to share all my opportunities and adventures I have common sense and realize that it would not be in my best interest. Here is a condensed version of a few highlights and major events. In January I transferred to college in Milwaukee to be near my brothers and amuse myself by observing their social life. I participated in intramural sports. I decided to participate in the selling of educational material door to door for my summer job...except I got stuck in Ohio. I learned loads of stuff and the sacred art of mooching was revealed to me which I perfected throughout these three months. I returned to college with high spirits and very bad tan lines. For my contribution to humanity I allowed myself to be used as an experiment for medical research. For Thanksgiving I hitched a ride to Boulder, Colorado (picked my sister up on the way) and tore up the slopes. After Christmas, at home, I transferred to a college in Minnesota having decided to become a teacher with a focus on English. The food is good and the rules are dumb. I leave my life to God and my whims.

MICHAEL: Since January of last year I have had a few large events happen in my life as well as the common difficulties we all face – like car problems causing headaches. First there was my trip to Jamaica where the rum is many flavors and the underwater world is crawling with curious creatures. During my second semester at school I heard of a former high school friend who made some great money, more than possible with any other summer job I have heard of to date. And so I joined the book field where much growth, maturity, responsibility and communication take place through selling door-to-door. I still have to make time for one weekend a month for the Marine Corps. I also have a cacoethes to tell some people about Jesus. I am in the midst of an enjoyable courtship. After Christmas I joined 500 college students in Nashville, Tennessee to learn more principles of *success* for the summer of bookselling and the rest of our life. It is also fun for me to critique such a humanistic organization. It has been a great year and I look forward to what 1999 will bring.

FREDERICK: I had the usual variety of conferences to attend. I continue to have classes with people interested in the church. In June I attended the national women's convention in Dallas and in July celebrated my 25th year in the ministry. I also had the privilege of returning to Wyoming in October to celebrate their 25th anniversary.. In September I accepted the position as district CCFS chairman. It's time consuming, but rewarding and it gets me out of town for meetings about every other month. My brother and family came for a visit which was a special treat and gave us a chance to visit Branson, Missouri.

JOANNE: Change. I could say it was a year of transition for me but then I wouldn't be in accord with the trend of using words that start with "C". So we'll go with change. Over Easter break our high school's traveling choir cruised to Phoenix, Arizona for our church's National Choral Fest. The highlights included visiting the Phoenix Police Museum and seeing a live scorpion after it died. I graduated in May and began corresponding with a college in Minnesota. My cherished boyfriend, who resides in Boulder, Colorado, commenced with boot camp at the USAF Academy in Colorado Springs. I spent the summer season in my clergyman's home carrying convenience foods on trays to parked cars, cross-stitching, and careening about the city on my cycle. At college I tried out and made the volleyball team. Classes were competent and classmates cordial.

PAUL: I continue to cohabit with Michael at college in Wisconsin where countless changes occur to improve the captivating atmosphere of the college. I am studying theology, chemistry, Spanish, and history…covering an array of courses…possibly to see how long I can attend classes instead of working at a real job. I can't justify the time commitment for a sport in college but work out with my Ucranian roommate on a regular basis. I am still a Corporal in the Corp but only work once a month in Green Bay. The cold weather training continues to be the most challenging occurrence carried out by the captains at the unit. The usual mechanical chores executed on the large cumbersome equipment is a welcomed ceasing to the college student's studious comportment. The money accumulated is also a decent incentive to carry on these cumbersome chores with a contemplative confidence, knowing little about what is being done. Over the summer I worked construction and the most I got out of that was a craving for more college education or conversing with others in a carefree college environment where causal conversation is not the exception.

ANYA: While I can't compete with clever college conversation I can correlate a few events from 1998. I continue to cohabitate with Frederick…you know, the guy with charisma and corny comments. We spent the commemoration of our wedding in Hot Springs. The entire clan was concurrently present for Frederick's 25th anniversary celebration. I enjoyed cruising the continental United States. A trip to Milwaukee with a friend afforded time with all the children except Thomas. Had several days to connect with friends and get a conception of children's college life. Reunion with Cheyenne chums was possible at the church's 25th celebration. Visited with Thomas a couple of times in Longview. Concluding trips to Waco in the Cornhusker State were for a "My Fair Lady" performance which Joanne took part in, and for the last high school commencement ceremony. We delivered the same child to college in Minnesota in August. I continue to accompany the congregation on the clavichord, work with children and ladies' choirs and serve as contact for the church's women's group. I constantly crave the competition of contract bridge and have succeeded in accumulating over twenty masterpoints which gives me the current title of 'Club Master'. Contemplating completion of my spelling series is a daily commitment. In conclusion, God has blessed us in abundance. I pray that all of our loved ones will be among the blest received into heaven.

THOMAS: Continuing my occupancy in this coveted country of Texas (confined citizens in the covered campestral corners of the state still haven't conceded Texas' annexation), the year was spent scrutinizing cerebral concepts, concentrating on cognizance, and concerning myself with building a computer business. Chronologically, the year commenced with the start of my first winter in Texas (January 9th, I think it was) and the end of winter, January 11th)! From this I concluded that the climate definitely compensates for any lack of cultivated civilization.

Come February I took an annual trip to Colorado to remind me of coldness, visited with friends, and skied the slopes. Other singular events of the year include studying karate, taking up contract bridge again, and playing softball. The clefts between these events were filled with the above diversions.

Marie spent some time with us after three years of college still not knowing what vocation to choose. Though Frederick had a better relationship with his daughter she finally became the sixth victim of his uncontrollable wrath. She had previously made some friends during summer months when she was home working. She met one of these friends at a movie theater. I was sick in bed. Paul was home for a short visit. Around 10:00 p.m., Frederick started wondering where his daughter was. Alas, while defending his sister, Paul dropped the information that the young man she was out with was black. Oh my goodness! Paul was sent to find her and tell her to get home... Now!!! He did find her and returned home to say the two of them were sitting in the young man's truck talking. Frederick allowed another thirty minutes to elapse. Finally he went himself. I can only imagine the scene and embarrassment my daughter felt. Frederick arrived home and daughter soon followed. A heated argument ensued between Frederick, daughter, and son. I listened from the bedroom. Finally the real issue was addressed...out with a black man? I could not believe what followed even knowing Frederick's mother definitely was prejudiced. No daughter of Frederick's would be with a black man. What if a church member would see her. Marie came back with wasn't evangelism even for blacks? Frederick stated that our church was not ready to accept a black visitor. I had to check the calendar to be sure I was hearing this in the twentieth century. I did not hear my daughter's response to this unbelievable statement but it earned her at least one good slap across her face. She did not speak to her father again and left two days later. It took me six months of writing letters and talking to her on the phone before she could forgive him and move on.

Newsletter (Wanted List) - 1999

(sorry, for anonymity I cannot post the really great 'mug' shots)

The FEC (Federal Evacuation Committee) mandates copies of this be posted in every bathroom!

Joanne: seen in Oklahoma selling books (educational?)...rumored to have extended meeting in Hawaii with boyfriend's family...seen in New York over New Years...spotted in Arkansas visiting parents...majority of time in Milwaukee attending classes at college.

Marie: Occasionally seen in a classroom at college...observed posing as a bridge caddy in San Antonio...spotted during summer with brother in Longview...brief visits reported in Arkansas..also seen in New York...twin fetish?? (babysitting three month olds in Longview and eighteen month olds in Milwaukee)...possible accomplice – Derek!

Paul: Also seen with book bags in Oklahoma...part of a wild Easter retreat in Arkansas...rumored to be in Michigan twice, once with a Ukranian and the other posing as a marine taking pictures of US helicopters!...crossed Texas border into Mexico over Christmas (accompanied by Jesus)...emergency records in Milwaukee indicated he was not spared from the 'intestinal revenge'.

Michael: Several trips indicated to Tennessee related to book selling management...also seen in Oklahoma...canoeing and 'cliff jumping' with group in Arkansas...posed as a marine for two weeks in California...spotted on a Colorado mountain with skis on...reported to have an RA position at college...may have more than one female accomplice (one with ties to Puerto Rico).

Thomas: strong leads to residency in Longview foiled by several sightings in Milwaukee...reason to believe from license plate he led the New York escapade...name listed with gold points in San Antonio National Championship Bridge results...identified with some WEB designing...school in Wisconsin?

Anya: cooks...cleans...irons...does seem to have wife status...Big party (possible 50 theme)...seen without husband in Wyoming (gang reunion)...name also seen in San Antonio Bridge results-though no gold points were listed...summer borders (booksellers) included an Ecuadorian.

Frederick: status-minister... residence-Arkansas ...tryglycerides-638! ...reported in numerous cities-Dallas, Orlando, Milwaukee, San Antonio (not bridge) always posing as a pastor...mostly travels alone but seen on occasion with a *beautiful* young woman (Orlando, Dallas, Houston and Milwaukee)...suspicious visit from Puerto Rican family. Though never seen all together at one time we are certain there is a connection between all of the above. Due to their frequent encounters and associations with *foreigners* they are all wanted for questioning. We suspect the leader may have noticeable problems as rumor has it that he and his chair fell of the riser while singing the first hymn on Christmas Eve. One also has to wonder if there is a plan sending a team of 5 to the same college in Wisconsin.

Frederick did finally join me in a once a month couples bridge club. We met at a restaurant first which he always balked at. He always hoped to get out of it but his small congregation did not demand much of his time. In spite of himself he enjoyed it.

The children's visits became less frequent and shorter. I realized I wrote way too much about them in my newsletters but I see now that I needed that time to focus on them and enjoy their pursuits. Frederick and I never had conversations of how proud we were of them. We never prayed for them. There were only verbal assaults on their choices and the way they spent money. Their adventurous personalities were my fault. I cared more about them than I did about him. Well, I couldn't argue with that.

Newsletter (Travelogue) – 2000

We begin our tour in HUNTSVILLE, ALABAMA, home to one of the three NASA space centers in the US. It is also the home of a church mission who used a summer TCW (travel canvass witness) team. Joanne was half of that team for the summer. Only two hours north is NASHVILLE, TENNESSEE. This was the site of the church's women's convention. Joanne was able to join her mother for the Saturday morning session, her 1st exposure to a convention. I rate this the best ever convention. The Steel Pan Band from Antigua definitely stole the show. Our group was responsible for aiding a fallen (fainted) member of this band. Heading due west we run into CAMP LEJUNE, NORTH CAROLINA, home of one of the three marine divisions in the world, the other two being in California and Japan. This is where Michael and Paul spent their two week summer duty. Traveling up the Atlantic coast we arrive in BOSTON, MASSACHUSETTS, to look in on Thomas and Marie, who moved there in October and December respectively. Thomas moved out to train as a manger and assistant general manager of a Tealuxe. He discovered via the internet there were nine new ones opening in Boston. Ah, what there is to know about tea, for instance; all tea comes from the same plant, Camellia Sinensis, a type of evergreen shrub. There are thousands of teas, a result of location and climate and processing. Marie followed as there was promise of a job as a "tea tender". She also found a part-time job in a fitness center. Now we must hop on a jet to go 3000 miles over the Atlantic to LONDON (a large city where they really do have a clock on top of a lot of bricks) where Marie made contact with a friend from college. Since they refused her entrance to Parliament she headed up to SCOTLAND, one of the most scenic areas of Europe. There has been no war here for more than 200 years. She spent a day on the ISLAND OF SKYE, just one of Scotland's hundred islands. Back in London she took a quick jaunt to the mountainous island of SARDINIA, ITALY, second in size of Mediterranean islands and one of Italy's leading cork producers...then back to London and then home all in six weeks. Catching a jet back to the U.S. we land at O'Hare in CHICAGO, a cross-through for many trips and also where the first ever Missionary Conference was held which Anya and Frederick attended. Well, we can't leave out MILWAUKEE – (we have a lot of money invested there). January to May we actually had all five children attending the same college! In the fall we were down to just Michael and Joanne and Michael teases us that he will actually graduate in May. The trusty old van was stolen in November and after the insurance company paid us it was found with contents still in it (except Marie's homemade quilt from her mother). Michael wrote a short piece on this...very funny. And Frederick still ends up in Milwaukee for CCFS (collecting currency for the synod) conferences. This was also the beginning of our 'vacation' as in just the two of us...after our Chicago meeting. We went around LAKE MICHIGAN spending time at the KITCH-IT-KIPPI springs, the world famous Soo Locks (the passage for ships

around the St. Mary River rapids) in SAULT STE MARIE –
very briefly touched CANADA, crossing the three mile bridge,
made it over to MACKINAC ISLAND (Fort Mackinac was
built by the British in 1780) and spent too short a time in
HOLLAND, (settled in 1847), touring De Zwaan windmill (the
last to leave the Netherlands), the DeKlomp wooden shoe and
Delft factory. Spring would be the time to return and immerse
oneself in tulips. GREEN BAY should be mentioned where
monthly marine duty is still carried out by Paul and Michael.
Going west we hit WILBUR, NEBRASKA, where Anya spent
a week loafing around. Further west we come to WYOMING,
specifically, CODY, established by Buffalo Bill, where Anya's
brother bought a home and property. Marie spent the summer
here watering gobs of plants, setting up trees knocked over by
'Maria', transplanting, pruning etc. Just before one hits Idaho is
the little town of ALPINE, south of JACKSON HOLE (now
contaminated by that visit from William Jefferson You Know
Who) where lives a kindly little old lady. Investigations over
voting fraud in Alpine are still underway!! Pauline, the little
old lady, will soon move to Cody where her son is renovating
an apartment within his house for her. Anyway, Michael and
friend spent the summer in this area doing landscaping jobs
for their uncle. CALIFORNIA – RANCHO CUCAMONGA
near Los Angeles is where Joanne spent spring break as part
of TCW team. LAS VEGAS, NEVADA – February CCFS
meeting held – wives welcome!!! The extravaganza of it all is
more than the eyes and feet can take in just a couple of days.
Also toured Hoover Dam, one of seven modern civil engineering
wonders. Construction was begun in 1931. We head back east to
BOULDER, COLORADO. Thomas was here for summer and
fall...was to be enroute to India but instead became an employee
of The Tea House and onward to Tealuxe in Boston. Straight
south just before leaving the U.S. we come to BIG BEND
NATIONAL PARK, so named for the big bend of the Rio
Grande. Michael, Marie and friends camped here over Spring
break. Not quite like the northern Rockies! We are leaving
the US again. We left Paul last year recovering from intestinal
bacteria from MEXICO but he went back in September for
more. He took a Spanish class in MONTERREY, one of
Mexico's largest cities, staying with a host family. Skipping some

classes he decided it more productive talking to people while traveling in cities such as SAN MIGUEL, a very old historic town, where he met many Mexican students who were eager to communicate with a Gringo as handsome as himself. In PUETO VALLARTA, a popular resort area on the Pacific coast, he met three young senoritas who happened to be studying Englishe… so the story goes. The senoritas were very willing to help him study Spanish. He also took in a bullfight. OKLAHOMA CITY, DALLAS and HOUSTON held pastoral meetings and conferences which Frederick attended. And finally home to the Republican state of ARKANSAS. We made it up to BELLA VISTA (a good place to retire if you enjoy bridge and golf) for a pastor installation. Frederick and I took a canoe ride down the Buffalo River in a canoe. MOUNTAIN HOME hosted a pastoral conference. LITTLE ROCK (home of you-know-who's library) is frequented for golf, shopping, and airport service. By the way, the city was absolutely breath-taking after the ice storm. The branches were so thick the ice could not be shaken off. It was like a glass city.

Our church had a fair booth this year handing out hundreds of information sheets. We also hosted the 2nd joint Reformation service. The most gala event of the year was the wedding between a member here and a former member of Nebraska. Frederick was finally talked into singing the Lord's prayer and of course he did a superb job. As one member stated afterwards, "you know, I always thought he had that in him." The following day for mission festival we featured the groom's brother-in-law from one of our missions in Russia.

Having completed her grade school spelling series, formatted on the computer by Thomas, Anya joined the Red Cross. She actually was called to set up a shelter after the first ice storm but no one showed. She did her civil duty working the polls…twice, and is waiting for royalty checks for use of a picture she sent in to The International Library of Photography. The picture title, "Girl on Edge of World" (starring Marie) is a semi-finalist in its category. Bridge? Oh, yes, she still plays.

Last stop – Heaven – the golden city, awaiting all the saints who nobly confess Jesus as their Savior. See you there if we don't run into you before!

Our vacation around Lake Michigan had some positive moments but way too many disagreements on choosing tourist sites and spending money. It certainly would have been beneficial to plan ahead. Las Vegas was better because we were with Fredericks's peers. They were *normal* in their desires to take in some sights even if it meant spending some money. Again…a great reality check for me.

The canoe ride down the Buffalo River left me wondering if Frederick's unbelievable outbursts of anger would some day kill him. The river was swift enough that it demanded constant maneuvering and paddling cooperatively. We were unable to avoid a low hanging bush and over we went. I managed to grab two items. Frederick came up with only himself. We made it to shore easily and the canoe was recovered not too far downstream. Taking stock of our losses, Frederick quickly realized his wallet and contents, which he had taken out in the canoe to dry after we were hit by the first wave, were gone. He turned red and his eyes bulged! He could not even begin to hide this from our fellow travelers. For a week he had to vent his anger over the ridiculous canoe trip we should never have taken in the first place.

Frederick demeaned my attempts to join volunteer organizations. I suspected pornography but had no proof. I lived in fear of the next outburst. Volunteering a couple times a week at the hospital and going to the gym several times a week helped me both emotionally and physically. I had had muscle and gastrointestinal problems for years with no satisfaction from doctors as to cause or cure. Sleep now became the major problem. Again, no support or interest from Frederick. And again my sinful reaction was anger, resentment and self-pity. As a result I took public opportunities to lash out or be unsupportive of Frederick, not intentionally so but statements just blurted out when there was a chance to vent my pent up feelings.

> When my soul was embittered, when I was pricked in heart, I was stupid and ignorant, I was like a beast toward thee. Nevertheless I am continually with thee; thou dost hold my right hand. Thou dost guide me with thy counsel, and afterward thou wilt receive me to glory.
>
> Psalm 73:21-24

I finally completed my grade school spelling series (I had been working on this for ten years) which Thomas formatted for me on the computer. Frederick took no interest. When I received my first order he offered no congratulations. In fact the day after the sale two cousins came for a visit and they celebrated with me. He did not join in. When I received my second order his comment was pointed at the teacher's folly and lack of discernment. Luckily two of my children were home and congratulated me.

Newsletter (Slivers of Truth) - 2001

Material made possible by Frederick (benevolent dictator), Anya (domestic goddess), Thomas, Michael, Paul, Marie, and Joanne

Deep in the woods lived a benevolent dictator and his domestic goddess. Since the dictator was mostly content to observe seeds sprout, his goddess often wandered off into the forest on her own. On an occasion in the midst of winter the mother of the goddess needed to be transplanted from her grove in a forest quite far off to a new grove not far away. Coincidently, the tundra-huggin' sister of the domestic goddess was able to join in this adventure as she passed through on her four-wheel sled accompanied by her daughter. After finishing the move and bidding the mother and brother Johnny Appleseed farewell, the trio left for the Dakotas to smoke-um peace pipe with brother Dan and tribe. On the way they stopped in Ten Sleeps for coffee…that would be ten sleeps from the winter camp and ten sleeps from the summer camp as the 'Paint' travels. Next the journey took the three South to Nebraska grain country and at last they returned to the forest home of the benevolent dictator.

Fortunately for the goddess the dictator felt rot and decay setting in so he took her to a far away country for an entire week. Palm trees were an exotic change as were beaches…Coqui frogs.. Pina Coladas…snorkeling…Bicardi tour (with samples)…. mission staff get-together…Puerto Rican Christians..Fort El Moro. All this plus mucho laughing and discussions with our friends and host. Finding it difficult to sway in the March wind after three months of grazing, the domestic goddess took up

Saturday lumbering through the woodlands. It was a challenge to keep up with people over eighty.

'Ere summer descended the woodsy couple with saps, Paul and Marie, attended Michael's graduation in Milwaukee. The longest part of the auto trip was Paul learning Slim Shady. On the last day of May, in the rain, with cash-in-hand, the benevolent dictator made an offer on a plum colored non-diesel car just perfect for the domestic goddess and it became hers! To add to the boughntiful year..the domestic goddess sold her first spelling series. Ahhh, the sweet nectar of success! The third sale went to her grade school alma mater in Cheyenne, Wyoming. That was special! An apartment blaze offered the domestic goddess a chance to do some actual work with the Red Cross. And thanks to a mild prescription drug the domestic goddess is able to saw logs on a regular basis. Sleep definitely reduces her bark.

About the time when leaves were dropping the benevolent dictator decided he could no longer blame his protruding trunk on the angle of the lens. And so began a series of life style changes…walking…increased watering…less pulp…running… slim fast…pushups…rice cakes…sit-ups…ordering salads at restaurants. He continues his treemendous work here for the Lord plus travels for CCFS and conferences. He was able on one such trip to Milwaukee to celebrate Joanne's twenty-first birthday.

On the germinating of the five saplings;

As of September, Michael, or Dad Jr., as Marie calls him, is in Fayetteville, Arkansas pruning his skills of logic and oration in Law School. There should be plenty of opportunity for meditation on the knowledge of good and evil. Joanne yodeled in the Alps on choir tour in Europe. She majors in English and has stumped her parents on occasion with her rhetoric. She blooms as a resident assistant, an office cleaner for an insurance company and a babysitter. Paul has many friends in Mexico, Neil the Mennonite farmer, and many senoritas. He spent a total of seven months split between Durango and Guanajuato, where he took four classes at the university. The summer was spent in Sheridan, Wyoming doing evangelism. He was arbored by a couple Frederick married in Cheyenne. Perhaps he will use his Spanish and Theology in the Dominican Republic after graduation in May. Thomas branched out, experiencing Italian cuisine and fruit of the vine in Italy with sister Marie. The Italians' slower pace of life appealed to him. He passed thru the homeland on his way to Boulder, Colorado where he worked a couple of months and then moved on to Milwaukee. As soon as his income increases he seems intent on pursuing a chef career. The angels rejoiced loudly with us this Christmas over Thomas's return to Christianity. Words cannot express the joy anymore than they could express the sorrow of three years ago. Our prayers will continue for those of you who are still suffering and awaiting the return of a loved one. Thank-you to all who prayed with us! God does listen! Marie kilt a fat calf but was unable to transport it over the Mexican border. The foliage of Maristan, a former country of short people according to Paul, acquired new colors in Italy, and Puerto Rico (knot to be outdone by her parents), and Mexico. She farmed with Neil, bonded with Paul in Guanajuato and rode horses with Cello, Paul's first senorita. She did stick close to her Ma and Pa fir a month and acorny time it was.

Der Tannenbaum took a lot of needling this year as it was only a Norfolk Pine with very not-impressive decorations...but it reduced the stress level for the domestic goddess who was determined to enjoy every moment of the first time in three years all the saplings (plus Neil, the Mennonite farmer from Mexico) would be home. There were also no presents...instead everyone planned a day...and the winner is...*Thomas*!

We had six wonderful surprise visits this year...good friend from Nebraska, cousins from Texas, first cousin once removed and family from Texas, High School friend and her husband, sister and son who is now training in Army special forces, and previous friends from Arkansas who have since moved to Wisconsin. These woods can get lonely...we cherish each and every visit.

We leaf all of our futures in God's loving hands. We pray He prunes as necessary to enable each of us to bear more fruit this year. And may we work on our own logs and not worry so much about our neighbor's splinters!

Sexual intimacy notably decreased. I had moved to a back bedroom to try and get some sleep with extra pillows etc. This in itself did not affect sexual intimacy. I do recall a night I awakened and on the way to the bathroom saw Frederick at the computer. He left before I exited the bathroom. I did not have a good feeling about this.

When the children were home for Christmas I was back in the master bedroom with Frederick. Even though he was not taking part in our family activities we were sharing sexual moments together until one night I curled up to his back and received no response. In twenty-six years there was always some response be it positive or negative. I shrugged it off. The next week I tried again…nothing! Though we had acquired few interests together over the years, engaged in limited outside activities together at least we were compatible sexually, except when there was extreme discord between us. Well, only two strikes, so a couple of weeks later I attempt once more to bridge the gap and encourage an amorous reaction…nothing!! Now I am shattered. This is not just a quirk. For some unknown, unspoken reason I am being rejected…shunned! This is an overwhelming feeling of the reality of being unloved. This feels more permanent, more hurtful, more intentional; this causes intestinal distress and obsessive anxiety. I am embarrassed but break down and tell my sister after the second and third attempts. It is extremely difficult to hear yourself say out loud that your spouse wants nothing physically to do with you. I mention my calls to my sister because eight months later during counseling Frederick lied about this time frame. I needed to be convinced yet one more time that this was reality and so a fourth attempt is made to obtain a reaction from him. How stupid and slow can we be?? I spend the next week telling myself what an idiot I am for setting myself up to be again rejected. Now I won't even respond to the slightest hint of physical contact lest I be rejected and hurt again. So the endless circle is set in motion. Perhaps there were tender moments on his part but I am in a 'you won't hurt me again mode' and therefore will not respond to anything. He, of course, always unable to express his feelings, never brings the subject up and so five months of a cold war pass with a pretense that there is some sort of warped marital bond when in fact there is nothing more than two people living at the same address, one expecting his lunch to be ready every day, his wash done, his shirts ironed, and mending done promptly; the other expecting nothing, simply going through the motions of everyday life wondering how long this earthly life will last.

In order to become more involved with The American Red Cross I signed up for a week long camp taking two classes a day. Somehow I got by with this. I now know he enjoyed his week alone! I don't think I ever realized over the years that a more controlled tone in my voice over a fearful one made a difference in what I would be allowed to do. Classes were mostly good but who needs a second round of dormitory life. Frederick knew when I was returning but I arrived early to find him naked in the kitchen doing dishes. This new naked thing was becoming a life style. So, the question was, now that I completed classes, what did I think I was going to do for Red Cross. The answer, take a three week deployment for a disaster. So much for that friendly reunion...in my face…red face…yelling!!

I suggested more counseling. He of course refused. Throughout this time I don't know if I ever thought of turning to another pastor for help. After all, bringing the church into the picture in Nebraska proved disastrous coupled with Frederick's threat that I better never do it again. Through all this time I asked if there was something he would like to do with me but there wasn't so I thought I might as well keep on with my separate life.

Meanwhile I had been invited by my sister to Alaska for an adventure on Kodiak Island. I had not seen her for seven years! She offered to pay whatever so Frederick could not prevent me from going with the money argument. I casually mentioned a trip to Alaska once just to feel him out and he laughed. It took me a month to muster up enough courage to tell my sister I would come. First I asked Frederick if he would consider a vacation in Alaska. He said, "I have no great desire to see your sister and her husband." As long as Frederick was already mad I told him I was going to visit my sister….I mean really, a person can only yell so loud and get so red and only so close to your face. We were in the car so I felt relatively safe. He questioned the expenditure of money but I had the reply of my sister's generosity ready. Actually my new life so overwhelmed him, he was actually too shocked to say much more than what did I think I was doing. My favorite was how many weeks did I think I could miss church, his church that is. When the time came to leave, however, he told me I couldn't go so I had to pack secretly and leave when he was at work. My son took me to the airport and I was off. Frederick called me after I arrived in Alaska and suggested maybe it was a good idea for us to have a vacation together and he was willing to fly up. I knew the details of our Kodiak trip would be too much for him and roughing it was definitely out of his league so I just said we had plans and it was a little late for the offer. He did not know my daughters were coming or that other family was joining us after the Kodiak adventure.

Back home routine life became more difficult. I felt myself plunging down a pit with no bottom. Being a codependent of an abusive relationship, this pit was not new to me but it was deeper and darker. I reached an all time low...spiritually, emotionally and physically. I found myself questioning God's promise not to give me more than I could bear. These feelings scared me.

> My heart is in anguish within me, the terrors of death have fallen upon me. Fear and trembling come upon me, and horror overwhelms me. And I say, "O that I had wings like a dove! I would fly away and be at rest; yea, I would wander afar, I would lodge in the wilderness, I would haste to find me a shelter from the raging wind and tempest.
>
> Psalm 55:4-8

In March I took a rare stand and said I was going to visit my mother. Partly I could say it because if he forbade me on monetary grounds my mother would pay for the trip. I spent two weeks with her instead of the usual one week. I dreaded returning!

More opportunities presented themselves for me. The first of my relatives (my great-grandfather) reunion in fifty years took place in Milwaukee, Wisconsin. All five of the children would be there. Frederick had no interest in being with a bunch of my relatives. In fact, he had forbidden me into several years of marriage to talk about my father's ministry. One of the children was home and I drove up with him. It was because of this son's presence that I was able to get away for the event. From there I flew to Las Vegas for the annual women's convention. I had not told Frederick about this as I knew he would come unglued and forbid me to go. I felt the inevitable anger afterwards was worth the spiritual experience.

After one major outburst I packed a suitcase the next day when he wasn't around and got out while I had the chance. I had no idea where I was going. I was petrified he might see me in town or return home right away, read the note I had left, and come after me. I knew it was crazy but kept looking in the rear view mirror to see if he was following me. It was far fetched that either of these would happen but that is what fear does to you. Exhausted with anxiety I finally stopped at a rest stop...and cried.

I gradually made my way up north stopping at friend's houses and realized how dependent I had become and scared to do anything on my own. I wasn't able to make a purchase. It was as though Frederick was with me watching everything I did. I didn't even know who I was anymore. At my first stop in Nebraska Frederick had already been in touch and left a message for me, "Tell her to turn the car around and get back home." He pestered me with phone calls which I didn't take because I knew I was just going to get an earful. My friend finally took one of his calls and told him he could e-mail me but I wouldn't take any calls right now and that I was not coming home. Pastors from the area emailed and called telling me to come home. I was a nervous wreck just imagining Frederick's anger and how could I ever go home and face him.

> But I am like a deaf man, I do not hear, like a dumb man who does not open his mouth. Yea, I am like a man who does not hear, and in whose mouth are no rebukes. But for thee, O Lord, do I wait; it is thou, O Lord my God, who wilt answer. For I pray, "Only let them not rejoice over me, who boast against me when my foot slips!" For I am ready to fall, and my pain is ever with me. I confess my iniquity, I am sorry for my sin. Those who are my foes without cause are mighty, and many are those who hate me wrongfully. Those who render me evil for good are my adversaries because I follow after good. Do not forsake me, O Lord! O my God, be not far from me! Make haste to help me, O Lord, my salvation!
>
> Psalm 38:13-22

On the way up north I stopped at our previous counselor hoping he would have a minute for me which he did. He reassured me I was doing the right thing and this gave me strength. He admitted he'd never held out much hope for Frederick to actively right the wrongs that led to our marital discord.

I then made my way to some friends in Iowa. I felt safer there. Frederick never figured out that they would be my next stop.

I continued north to a dear friend in Mankato. She had just retired from teaching and was packing to move. It was great therapy for me to help her pack. What a blessing to have so many scattered friends. God knows our future far ahead of us. At times I was disheartened at not having roots. Perhaps you do and local friends and family will be there to sustain you. I have met women from domestic violence situations who remain in the same town as their abuser and even see them at church or every week exchanging children. More power to them. I really can't imagine doing that.

I contacted one of our synod counselors in Milwaukee and was told we could meet with them. I e-mailed Frederick and suggested the counseling in Milwaukee. Of course he really had no choice if he wanted to keep his ministry intact. I arrived in Milwaukee and checked into a motel, courtesy of the church body. Frederick thought this very presumptuous of me. I attended the closest church the following Sunday and there I found a Pastor who willingly met with me immediately after church. He was extremely empathetic and consoling. I wondered if he knew of anyone with an extra room where I could stay since it was going to be an extended stay. He listened to my story (I was very emotional) and did not think I was crazy. I was worried about this as Frederick had often told me I was and had often uttered this diagnosis to my friends and family. At this time I was not thinking anything permanent but enough time that Frederick would really work at coming to terms with his sins of abuse and sexual immorality and that he would take my needs seriously. I think I had this hope because I still cared for him and wanted to believe that deep down he did have some feelings for me but I was determined to hold out until I felt our life together would change.

We had counseling for a week and it was intense. Most of the time we met together with a male and a female counselor. Several times we met alone, me with the female and Frederick with the male. Frederick felt very pressured and upset that he could not control the direction discussions took and did not like their suggestions. No assignment we were given worked out. Again we were advised not to live together. We were told to have a date and not discuss issues. We went to dinner. This was what I longed for, to be alone with my husband enjoying each other's company. Conversation was awkward but went alright. After the next session he was upset over a possible impression I had left with the counselors and he would not drop it. Our next assignment was to set up a budget. He read three newspapers at the library (he lied about this to the counselor) while I found a book to get started and asked him for information. When I had gleaned information from him and came up with a budget he informed me I had to abide his decisions on money; that was part of his headship and his family values would rule and besides some of the money we were talking about came from his mother and there would be no discussion on that (he always referred to the money as his, in fact corrected one of the children for thanking me for some money... it wasn't from me, it was *his* money). The next day the counselor tried to get Frederick to agree to grant me some spending money each month - no questions asked. The counselor started at $100 and worked his way down to $50 after Frederick responded no to each amount. No way! Then we were told to spend a night together. As soon as we were in the motel room he turned on the TV. I asked if we could go down to the hot tub. He didn't want to. I suggested we talk. He watched TV. I went to the hot tub. I tried again to talk when I returned. He was upset about counseling. We agreed not to spend the night and I left. The week of counseling was almost over and I could see no progress. Pornography was brought up. Frederick vehemently denied there was any (I now know that to be a lie but have promised not to reveal the source).

At this point the counselor stated that he had never seen spouses so determined not to forgive each other. He asked Frederick first if he could forgive me. He said yes. Then it was my turn. I asked Frederick what he would like to be forgiven for...the counselor came to the edge of his seat, raised his voice, waved his arms, and stated all of Frederick's sins for which I should forgive him. It wasn't that I did not understand Jesus' command to forgive seventy times seven times but it bothered me that up to this point Frederick had denied or minimized all sins against our marriage. I did verbally forgive Frederick but the incident forever left me baffled. Finally ten years later after a sermon on forgiveness and a talk with the pastor I know how that scene should have played out. The counselor dropped the ball by not asking Frederick to confess his sins...this was a matter of spiritual priority. Since he didn't do it I should have intervened and asked Frederick again which sins he wanted me to forgive, not that I needed to know but again for his spiritual welfare. I would forgive him whether he told me or not. Did not denying or minimizing his sins show lack of contrition? Only when one confesses his sins and feels crushed under the weight of them can one realize the magnitude of God's forgiveness. While this work of the Holy Spirit is daily and personal, when a sin is committed against a fellow Christian, especially in a marriage, confession and then forgiveness must take place.

Frederick and both counselors pressured me to return home and work on the list of issues we had made. I had asked for devotions as the number one priority. We had never had a devotion. We never brought our problems to the Lord. We never prayed together. He told the counselors he was uncomfortable having devotions with his children. I had therefore done them myself since the children were little. He made no comment on the two of us having devotions. I could not understand how going home at this point was a positive solution. We had failed all assignments. I suggested at the very least we needed a follow-up counselor in Arkansas. We agreed on a pastor. Frederick was angry…"I hope you're happy now that I've been raked over the coals!" We had not spent a night together. I decided to stay in Milwaukee and asked that we have daily talks over the phone. We had several that went ok and then he didn't have time to talk anymore. It was vacation bible school week and he was way too busy, too busy to make our marriage a priority.

After another week I was tired of living out of a suitcase and lost as to what to do next so I started making my way back home….one of many examples why we, the abused, cannot sever that tie and determine to make it on our own. The first night I stayed in a motel. The second day I went to Memphis and stayed with friends. From there it was an easy trip to pick up my sister from the airport on my way home. She just happened (that means the Lord was planning my life) to be coming from Alaska to see her son at Fort Campbell. We arrived home late. Frederick did not get up to greet me… oh well. I slept in my room down the hall. On my way home I had decided there was nothing else to do but make the best of things. I was resolved that this was not a conditional coming home but it was forever (otherwise how could I give it my all). The next morning I was out on the porch having a cup of coffee and all of a sudden Frederick got in his car and drove off. When he returned for lunch there was not even a glance in my direction. I took a chance and made the first move. I marched over to the couch where he was sitting and sat on his lap. His hands remained at his side and he ignored me as best he could. Not defeated I arose and offered him some lunch. I was invisible but he acknowledged my sister's presence and lightly conversed with her. Afterwards he went to the bedroom to lie down. I followed him and lay on top of him thinking maybe it was my sister's presence holding him back. He had said he wanted me to come home! No reaction. I rolled off and as I lay next to him feeling totally defeated, my hand brushed against his. He did not pull away but he had no response. I left. The next day we had counseling with the chosen pastor/counselor in Arkansas. I related my reception upon returning home. Frederick insisted we had held hands, not once, but he repeated it and repeated it. Unbelievable!! Later I confronted him again and reminded him the counselors in Milwaukee said it was up to him to regain my trust. I asked him if he was purposely punishing me for the counseling in Milwaukee and not immediately returning home. He admitted he probably was. He finally consented to e-mailing our new pastor/counselor in Arkansas and admitting he had lied about our holding hands. Even so I was an emotional basket case not knowing what to do next. Frederick was leaving the next day for a meeting in Milwaukee. I suggested our marriage was more important than a church meeting, ha! He left and I rearranged the whole house like a crazy person with my sister trying to calm me down and get me to face the reality of the last two days. Finally she found a box and started packing my frog collection...a little humor inserted into the situation. The following morning she packed a suitcase for me. I talked to Frederick on the phone and said I would not be there when he got home.

On the road again! First we went to Fort Campbell so my sister could check on her son who was having depression problems. Not knowing what to do next I called the pastor/counselor in Arkansas and of all things his in-laws were on vacation and we could stay in their house. This gave me a chance to settle down and have meetings with the pastor, though they were not very productive. I relaxed and began to find a peace I had not known in twenty-six years. I realized my sin of enabling Frederick rather than confronting his sins and helping him. I realized I had perfected martyrdom and wallowed in self-pity harboring anger and resentment. I cried to the Lord for forgiveness and the most wonderful peace descended on me... knowing that Jesus had gone to the cross for these sins and forgiveness was there. We then traveled around Arkansas looking for some place I could stay. Once again the Lord provided. I ended up at a Bed & Breakfast an hour from home. The owner agreed to a very discounted price once I related my circumstances. To show my appreciation I helped her with breakfast (even did it myself once when she was sick) and did some cleaning. My son Michael purchased a cell phone for me. Frederick would later question the necessity of that purchase.

I did not trust Frederick to make arrangements to see our pastor counselor every week (he was over an hour away) so I asked that he find a counselor in Russellville which he amazingly did. Actually it was probably much easier for him than meeting with a younger peer. We had several sessions that were ok. The good news was Frederick related well to this counselor, a former pastor. The bad news was after several sessions they would enter into a theological discussion which of course Frederick preferred over counseling. The main emphasis of this counselor was for the two of us to spend some time alone together everyday away from the house. This didn't happen but I finally moved back home. Every week the counselor asked how we were doing. I said we had done nothing together. The counselor said we should. Every week the same story. We did see the other pastor counselor twice more and studied a husband and wife's role in the marriage. During one of these sessions Frederick became agitated (rare in front of other people). He excused himself to go to the bathroom during which time the pastor asked me what level this display of anger was on a scale of one to five. I stated just getting into a three; he had a long ways to go to get to a typical outburst. After that session Frederick had no time for the next seven months to meet with this pastor. I emailed the pastor/counselor after an angry outburst. I called on another occasion for help. There was no help or even a response to the e-mail. I turned to the local counselor on my own once after an outburst from Frederick. He listened but that is all.

There did seem to be less ogling or maybe he was just more careful. At first he followed the suggestion to win back my trust giving me specifics of his whereabouts. But each week it seemed there were more and more unexplained gaps in the time frames he gave me.

One day I went over to church, as was my custom, to practice organ for Sunday services. I remember wondering why the study blinds were closed… not a usual circumstance. I unlocked the door (he often left it locked). The study door was closed (was easier to keep room cool). I tried the door and to my amazement it was locked. I heard "oh shoot" and then I heard him putting on his pants and the sound of a belt buckle and finally a ding (leaving a computer site?). I called his name and asked what was going on...no answer. I don't remember how long I stood there or how long I wandered around, I just remember I felt out of myself, panicky. I was there to practice organ. I tried but could not concentrate. I called Frederick's cell phone and heard it ring in the study. I tried the office phone...still no answer. I left figuring he would not come out as long as I was there. I was crazy with despair. I pulled over at a hotel and called my sister. That calmed me down a little and I returned to the church. There he was coming from the back wooded area to a rear church door. I went inside to find the study door opened. There was Frederick in the kitchen area just beginning to drink a glass of pop. I knew it would do no good to blow up. He was a master at playing this game. He said he had gone for a walk. Why did he lock his study door? Because the back door lock was difficult to work. *But if it was difficult wouldn't it be harder for someone to break in?*..Why did he have a sweater on I thought to myself. He was always on the hot side and then I remembered that other swooshing noise I heard in the study...oh yeah, putting on a sweater. Actually for someone who sweated just walking outside, he looked like he had just showered and dressed as in the morning. No, he did not have time from the time I saw him until I entered the opposite door to go down the hall, unlock his study door, go to the kitchen and pour himself a glass of pop complete with ice and why would he first bother to unlock the door if thirst was his priority. Anyway, you see how one can go crazy trying to figure out what is real, what might just be perceived, and what is total manipulation from the offender. And for these reasons I pursued the subject no further. I drove to the counselor's office. The counselor's response was that he was sure I was not imagining things and that I should use the guilt that Frederick would now have to get him to take me to a movie. A movie?! I had no time for the counselor after that.

Another pastor briefly entered my nightmare. He called to talk to Frederick who was not home at the time. It was a low day for me and I could not hide my emotions when the pastor inquired how I was doing. We talked to some length. At first I was reluctant to give to many details as he was a good friend of Frederick and of course I had good reason to believe the information could backfire on me. I assumed though that he would have some knowledge of my marital problems. He did not. He was empathetic which I needed at that moment. He said he would be glad to counsel us but I would first need to get permission from our other pastor/counselor.

Still no one was confronting the seriousness of the sins destroying our marriage. I felt alone and knew not where to turn for help. Looking back it would have done me a world of good to stay at a women's shelter and find out I was among many bewildered and lost abused women.

Another friend of Frederick's came down from the north to speak at our mission festival. Conversation at one point came to Alaska where he had also visited. Then there was talk of being involved with Church Volunteers, the sending out of lay people. This all connected and he suggested with my nursing experience I might try a Christian Camp in Alaska. What could Frederick say? This was a peer suggesting what he considered a normal undertaking but to Frederick was an idea from outer space.

Outside activities especially set him off if they interfered with his meals. Angry outbursts often ensued. Silly me, I thought once and a while he might grab a leftover or make a sandwich. I wondered why I had to have lunch prepared by 12:00 p.m. when he might not show until an hour later. The answer: his scheduled varied but his desire was to eat at noon, therefore the meal should be ready. He did offer to give me the courtesy of a phone call when he knew he was going to be late. If I was playing bridge or volunteering I was to leave a note telling him what there was for lunch.

Another meeting with counselor. We discussed time management and each other's priorities. This seemed to go well enough. In fact we continued the discussion on our way to the store and on our way home. I was comfortable enough that I expounded on priorities we each had which meant nothing to the other person. Then I made the fateful reference to lawn care as an example of a task he considered very important and for me it was on the bottom of my list. Actually, he never heard what was said after lawn. He escalated in seconds to a level five blow up. Arriving at home, I quickly left the car and went to the front of the house. We did not always lock the door but this time it was locked. I waited a few minutes then went around to the back again to get into the house. I grabbed the keys to my car and met him as I was coming out the door. He blocked my path and began yelling and waving his arms. I stood my ground for the first time and told him to quit yelling at me. He yelled louder! I repeated myself. He raised his arm and said he would do more than yell…in a brief second I think he realized he was exposed to the scrutiny of the neighbors and did not follow through. I got into my car, started it, and made it a few yards before it died. He had anticipated my flight and disconnected something. I got out and walked a few blocks to a friend's house. I was upset to the point of shaking and not able to make much sense. I stayed overnight.

The time had come. I was beaten down. I was exhausted. Michael had been on stand-by for months. All I had to do was give him the call to come and help me. I had no idea what the outcome would be but I knew this could be long term. Separation was in my mind. I did not yet see divorce as the ultimate answer. I started packing. Frederick had gone to the church. Michael came down from college and personal items rapidly filled the two vehicles. When we were nearly finished I placed my call to Frederick informing him of my intentions as I had promised the year before that I would not sneak away again. He was home in ten minutes. First thing on his agenda was to dismantle my car. Arguing commenced. Interestingly enough, Michael, as well as his siblings, had never really witnessed a major conflict between us. His surprise was obvious by the fact he called the police. Frederick turned into a sweet, mushy melon, the second the officer came into the house. Alas, the officer could do nothing about my vehicle as it was on private property and was marital property. The officer left and Frederick insisted I sit for just ten minutes and talk. He pelted me with questions usually giving the answers before I responded. I was determined not to kindle flames which was not hard as worn down as I felt. At one point he asked what percentage I saw each of us contributing negatively to the marriage. I shocked him with my response of 95% for his contribution. I explained the command for him to love me relegated him to a position of concern for my welfare and happiness over and above his. Well, of course this concept was a foreign matter he quickly rubbed out of his eye. Meanwhile my son repaired my car, parked his a half mile away, and then returned on foot. We left! My son went back up north to college. I stayed in a motel, courtesy of the American Red Cross.

The motel lay between our house and the church. I was scared to death Frederick would just happen to look into the parking lot and see my car. The next day I went to the bank and removed half of our funds, yes, this time I listened to the voices of family and friends saying I had no idea what he would do. In retrospect, of course I should have taken all but ten dollars which is what he left in the account the day after I departed the city. I contacted a few friends and said goodbye. The second day I was sure I saw Frederick's car pass. What would he do if he found me?? The next morning as I was getting into my car I felt there was something changed. Yes, there was a registration paper on the seat. I panicked. I looked in the back seat and saw some pop I did not remember putting in. I questioned my sanity and could not think straight. I was frantic to leave town.

In these last days it never crossed my mind to contact the circuit pastor. Had he served us? No one seemed to take seriously the accusations of abuse and sexual immorality. Why would anyone listen now except to tell me leaving and separation were wrong. No, I felt very much on my own. I just wanted to start running and not stop until I was worn out and could go no further.

I followed my son to his university town. He had found me a room with some Christians who helped people in need. On my bed was a copy of A Purpose Driven Life. I read the book over the next few days and felt refreshed with God's love and promises. "The Lord will fulfill his purpose for me: thy steadfast love, O Lord, endures forever." (Psalm 138:8). I had already purchased a ticket to Alaska to work at the Christian Camp as a nurse. My son took me to the airport. Once in the air I felt safe and free. The group of Christians I worked with at the camp was amazing. One in particular befriended me knowing from her past how difficult life could be maintaining balance and just putting one foot in front of the other. I was refreshed with God's word every morning during the staff devotion. Here I also met another lady whom God would use in the future to befriend me.

I had time between camp sessions to spend with my sister and family and my daughter, Marie, who had moved to Alaska after our great Kodiak adventure. My daughter and I made the trip north to Denali (Mount McKinley to outsiders). We tented in an abandoned camp site (neither of us had money). My night was a total nightmare of how best to distract a bear and obtain the safety of our car. After having breakfast in Talkeetna we hit a major traffic jam. We walked a mile past cars, campers and trucks to the site of the accident. Worse experience ever! A helicopter was just arriving to airlift two victims out. Seven experienced motorcyclists met head on by an elderly man who had dozed off while driving. I still feel sick just thinking of it…but I digress…this belongs in another book. Anyway, we saw Denali

Peak which percentage wise is really lucky. We took the bus tour through the park and saw every wild life species that inhabits the park.

There were many lonely hours though where I sat at my sister's table and played solitaire. I knew not the future and was depressed just at the uncertainty of it all. When camp ended I determined to deplane in Chicago and forfeit the remainder of my trip back to Arkansas. I took a bus to Milwaukee and spent some time with daughter, Joanne, and her husband. I had tried to spare my children a lot of details surrounding the demise of the marriage but they had questions and rightly so since our belief was that marriage was until death do you part. To help my daughter understand my separation I finally had to expose more details and this left her shaken. So sad! While in Milwaukee I met with the previous female counselor. She helped me organize my thoughts and come up with a list of conditions which would enable me to return to the marriage. I emailed these to Frederick. Two of the conditions were that he would obtain counseling for anger and pornography and be willing to spend at least a couple weeks with me, preferably with counseling. He never answered!

I had no car so I took a bus to an old high school friend's house. Twas a wonderful reunion seeing many old friends and relatives even with a dark cloud hanging over my head. Next I bussed to relatives in the twin cities. My brother-in-law surprisingly expressed empathy for me dragging around two suitcases making my way across two states. Surprising because he would later side with those who felt I had no cause for separation. And finally once again I took the bus to my friend who had told me I would always have a place with her.

My friend was a Christian and saw me through the initial shock of being on my own. I had no idea if this was going to be a permanent separation but I knew short term had not been successful. Through a previous counseling experience I had a number to call for a referral in my area. This and the steps to follow were all equally difficult. But I made the call. The counselor was two hours away. It was now obvious that long term at my friend's house was not the answer but first I would meet the counselor. He was great!! He promoted confidence by informing me I was in the less than five per cent of abused women who had the courage to leave their husband. Wow! He said I was well on my way to working through the steps one must go through in the face of loss. That is how much fear and lack of self-confidence we have after being yelled at, physically assaulted, and/or demeaned on a regular basis. The Lord had already helped me through the first difficult steps and that Fatherly assistance would continue to show itself time and time again in remarkable ways. Do not doubt that you are more important to him than the lilies of the fields.

I was able to meet Michael and retrieve my car. The future loomed ahead of me like a dark abyss. Playing games with my friend passed the time for awhile but I knew I had to make new arrangements.

Now realizing that this counselor was my main stay on the road to recovery, I packed and moved to the town of my counselor. This could only happen because again the Lord was in charge of my circumstances. Paul, after graduating from college, came to this town to continue his education in biblical languages. However, after his first year, being a marine reservist, he was called to active duty in North Carolina. His basement room was empty. The landlady gladly took me in, was a supportive Christian, and became a friend. Oh, it was not ideal as she rented the other two bedrooms in the basement to mentally handicapped men. She did offer her bathroom upstairs for my use for which I was very grateful. And so began my new life in Minnesota.

> I love the Lord, because he has heard my voice and my supplications. Because he inclined his ear to me, therefore I will call on him as long as I live. The snares of death encompassed me; the pangs of Sheol laid hold on me; I suffered distress and anguish. Then I called on the name of the Lord: "O Lord, I beseech thee, save my life!" Gracious is the Lord, and righteous; our God is merciful. The Lord preserves the simple; when I was brought low, he saved me. Return, O my soul, to your rest; for the Lord has dealt bountifully with you. For thou hast delivered my soul from death, my eyes from tears, my feet from stumbling. I walk before the Lord in the land of the living.
>
> Psalm 116:1-9

MINNESOTA
the church, recovery

This is my story of recovery from impending emotional and spiritual death. I have left Frederick and see no hope for reconciliation. I am scared, lost, bewildered, angry, and many more adjectives. My Christian counselor begins to help me put the puzzle together.

After the check bounced for my first counseling session I tried paying with a credit card and found out that it had been cancelled. I called the credit card company and found out it had been cancelled the day after I left home. Frederick had lied about this claiming it was the following week on advice from his counselor. I really looked forward to my counseling sessions. I began journaling as he suggested. My counselor strongly suggested I get a job, not just because I needed money but so I would have a reason to get out of bed on those mornings when the future looked bleak. Well, I hadn't actually searched out a job since before I was married and then, being a nurse, the search was easy. Having moved to so many states, I had not kept up my nursing license and had no desire to return to school.

Phone contact with friends and family became my social life. Regrettably, I found out that Frederick had also been calling my friends and family looking for support for his quest to prove my mental and emotional instability.

Emails continued between Frederick and myself. Taking the money out of our account was a "covert" action on my part. There were many inconsistencies and even contradictory statements from him. Anything he had done in the past was referred to as "marital struggles" or "acts that in themselves are not God pleasing." Never were they referred to as sins. Even so he stated these acts "cannot be compared to separating from the spouse." He stated his desire to work on our marriage but I would have to return in order for that to happen. Sometimes he sounded so sincere that for brief moments I entertained the idea of returning. Reality check! For twenty-six years he thought our marriage was fine and that I just needed to get a grip. There were many statements regarding my health. I was encouraged to find out what was wrong with me as my physical problems most certainly affected a healthy relationship in the marriage.

I began attending a church in town. I thought it strange after a month that the pastor never asked to speak to me so I brought up the possibility of a meeting and he confirmed this was on his agenda. The meeting went poorly. He had no empathy for my predicament. Alas, he knew Frederick and was all about us getting back together. Sometime later, when the district president from Frederick's area was in town, this same pastor asked to have another meeting with me in the presence of this district president. My son, Paul, was in town and he came with me. I had written up a brief summary of what led to my departure from the marriage as I knew I would be extremely nervous in front of these two pastors. I was shaking as I read it. The meeting was a disaster. The local pastor insisted I have yet another round of counseling with him and of course Frederick. I stated that I saw no purpose in this as we had already been through several counselors and the sessions had changed nothing. He then rose and strongly declared he would no longer give me communion. What? My son had been speaking on my behalf throughout and now called into question the legitimacy of this declaration on the basis of scripture. The district president said nothing. That was the end of any communication between myself and this local pastor.

Meanwhile I was taking care of seemingly menial tasks like opening a checking account and obtaining a new driver's license etc. All of these steps taxed my weak ability to function on my own. I had been home bound for so long with Frederick taking care of all paperwork and finances, I felt like a twenty year old starting out in life except I did not have the stamina or eagerness of a twenty year old. I felt I was beneath other adults socially. I feared they would find out my ignorance and lack of ability to cope in the world.

About this time I realized in an uncomfortable panicky sort of way that I was looking forward to my next counseling session way more than I should. The counselor was single, having lost his wife many years before. He was interesting and very easy to talk to. Obviously I had not settled on a divorce yet so this felt very wrong. I quickly sent him a letter saying any more meetings with him at this time would be unhealthy for me. However, I believe these feelings served a great purpose. It is all too easy to develop an intense dislike for the male side of our race. Having some feelings for my counselor kept me from sinking into this hole and made me feel alive…a step above zombie.

Friends are truly one of our greatest blessings. I contacted a friend from high school whom I had only seen a few times in thirty years. Eight years later we continue our new found friendship. She was and is always there for me and I know she sends prayers heavenward on my behalf.

> Journal entry, October, 22, 2003:
> Being attentive to doors opening or closing is perhaps the secret to moving on in a definitive direction. Truly trusting in the Lord means not being discouraged when a door closes but checking elsewhere in the house to see if a window is open – though it be the smallest crack. An open invitation through a door would be easy certainly but most often we are presented with just that crack in the window. Then it is up to us to put forth the effort needed to raise that window sufficiently, enabling us to take in the breath and sights made possible by entering this new dimension. Some windows don't open; they are stuck; the necessary tools to open a stubborn window may not be at your disposal. One must accept this…move on…there are many windows and doors. Certainly, do not pass by an open door on your search for an openable window!

I was very alone in my new city except by chance (which always means under God's direction) there was one lady, Bertha, whom I had worked with at the Christian camp in Alaska. After contacting her she took me under her wing. She was interning as a staff minister at the larger of our two churches in town. When I met her at church one day to go out to lunch, she introduced me to the head pastor. She immediately gave a brief description of my circumstances and left us alone. The pastor soon put me at ease and we had the first of many discussions. He became my savior, small s I always reminded him.

Bertha was graduating from college at the age of sixty-two. Since she was graduating mid-term she had to wait until spring for a call to serve in a church. She decided to spend the winter with her daughter. For our farewell lunch she took me out to a new Tea Room in town. The place was packed. When the waitress/owner finally came to our table and first of all apologized for the wait, I asked if her establishment needed help. She thought that might be a good idea. I brought my resume the next day, met with the owners the day after, and had myself a waitress job. The miracles just kept pouring in.

I was continuing meetings with Pastor S. I also had my landlady I could confide in and she included me in some of her circles. With Bertha spending the winter with her daughter, her apartment would be empty. She offered this to me and of course I accepted. It was a low housing rental which suited me perfectly. I hated to leave my landlady, but of course she understood and we did actually continue to keep in touch with each other.

I found out there was bridge at the senior center. After playing a few times, I was asked to substitute at a home. My first partner was a very vivacious friendly lady and we played well together. Some time later we met for lunch and became good friends. She and her husband saw me through the emotional traumas of the next several years.

I contacted the local American Red Cross. I was invited to a meeting. With hesitation I spoke up once and my offering was pleasantly received. I remember this as a turning point. I had been led to believe by Frederick that I had nothing worthwhile to say or add the few times I ventured out into the world. It was the usual demeaning. I did not have to endure that pitfall after this meeting. I felt wonderful! I felt free! I felt worthwhile! It was a monumental step in my healing process.

The Tea Room became my life. The décor of the Tea Room was antique sophistication. Workers had to wear dresses/skirts and a fancy apron. My Christian employer, Karen, became my friend. What wonderful long talks we had. She let my creative personality have wing. I soon knew her entire family. Over the next two years all five of my children and daughter-in-law worked the tea room during their visits. I had such fun helping to plan special events and organize how we would serve large groups like the "Red Hat" ladies. I received plenty of praise and compliments. April Fool's Day was such a success people stopped me on the street to tell me how much fun they had. My confidence was building and I had some self-esteem.

I had to come to Karen's rescue once when her husband went down the wrong path which would destroy their marriage. My daughter, Marie, was staying with them at the time and called me that evening. At first I thought she was pulling my leg….it just couldn't be. My poor daughter, bless her heart, she did a fine job of consoling until I arrived. Amazingly, before

Karen's husband fell off the cliff at the end of this path, he repented and with God's help planted his feet once again on solid ground. He accepted full responsibility and lovingly did everything to show his repentance was real. It is possible! I reflected on the reality of how totally opposite Frederick's path had been and still was. I met another man once who had also returned from a sinful life to his marriage. He began a speaking career with the intent of turning men away from sinful acts that destroy a marriage.

The church also became a part of my life. But I chose how I wanted to serve. I wasn't pressed into action as I had been with Frederick. As Pastor S. counseled me the marriage progressed to doomed failure. My emails became more matter of fact. Pastor S. advised me not to get into a debate. My suggestions for retrieving the marriage fell on deaf and unwilling ears – no surprise there. Frederick's emails often displayed a frantic person losing control. I was constantly asked for the name of my counselor, the doctor whom I was seeing, and the drugs I was taking.

My anger nagged at me; anger at the person who didn't love me and even now did not seem to care if I had money to support myself. This anger intensified as I used it to lash out at others. It took its form as jealousy of happily married couples and again self-pity when friends and relatives moved on to other life discussions that at present were unattainable for me. This has definite similarities to grieving the death of a loved one but alas the closure is not defined. Nightmares plagued me. My father had once told me that perhaps God sends us nightmares to aid us in working through our worst fears. In my nightmares I was often in some confinement with no means of escape. Gradually, the nightmares decreased and then were gone.

All money had been cut off to me the day after I had left. Luckily I had listened to friends and family and taken a few thousand out of our checking account. Obviously this couldn't last long and so the job was a necessity. The apartment was a low-income establishment and I could minimize on groceries as I ate some meals at the tea room and always took the leftovers that were destined to become garbage. The Lord gave me my daily bread as promised. However, I had to be practical and see that financial stability was shaky.

One day, the latter part of 2003, on a whim I turned into an attorney office building. Shaking and stammering I told the secretary I needed to see an attorney. He was wonderful and calmed me down. Divorce, though uncomfortable, seemed the answer at this point. I felt right with God so far as just cause for this action. Frederick's refusal to show love culminating in emotional abuse with the threat of physical abuse and refusal of marital sex voided the marriage. He had not gone for anger or sexual counseling and had done nothing to entice me home. His refusal to support me just added another log on the fire. The final result was petitioning for a legal separation which meant I would receive either monthly support or a one time settlement. I felt good leaving out divorce.

My son, Paul, was discharged from the marines just weeks before he would have been sent to Iraq and all discharges would be cancelled. Thank-you again Lord. Not that I wasn't ready to take my turn as a mother praying for her son's safe return. He returned to school and we were able to have some time together. Daughter Marie came to visit. This was one of those particularly low points for me. My attorney kept pushing Frederick but he was dragging his feet. He finally employed an attorney but still tried to control and even called my attorney once who promptly told him to go through his attorney. My two children decided I needed to get away. We traveled by car to Mexico. We were welcomed in by Paul's friend and family whom he had met on one of his independent travels in Mexico. We had a glorious time. The trip back was long and interesting. In Texas Paul was stopped by a policeman (who had already called for reinforcement) who became very upset when Marie photographed him. He also did not care for Marie and I helping Paul answer questions. So Paul was taken outside of our hearing. Well, the long and short of it…Paul was driving an old car… it was very dirty…and we were traveling north from Mexico…yep, drugs! They finally gave up and we were on our way. He was stopped again in Oklahoma and again in Nebraska (not for drug searches). We gave him a very hard time about this.

The summer of 2004 son, Paul, was in Mexico. He had been there many times before even taking a semester of college there. While pursuing his education he met a young woman whom he had kept in contact with off and on. This last time there he found her again and in months decided she was the woman for him. The family made plans to travel down for the wedding. This would be the first time I had seen Frederick since I left, eighteen months earlier. He was the last to arrive so I was settled in the home of my future daughter-in-law and surrounded by children. On the day he arrived and was expected at the home, I suddenly felt ill like my body was just shutting down. I went up on the roof (homes are built up the hillside) and became panicky, not a usual state for me. My daughter, Marie, sat with me and became concerned. I felt nauseated. Finally with some deep breathing (and a smoke) I relaxed and the feeling subsided. Down below we could hear Frederick had arrived. I had to get it over with. The greeting on my part was courteous without emotion. He was all smiles. I kept my distance to maintain my equilibrium. He never tried to pull me aside to talk with me about the past, the future, or anything. He did, however, invite his children to breakfast the next morning. Only two went. Ah, he had an agenda...discuss my problems with the children. His angry eyes met me at the wedding. He seemed very tired. I made no pretense of being with him and he didn't scare me! He insisted on sitting next to me at the wedding reception, very uncomfortable. I escaped quickly once the dancing started and was not with him again.

Shortly after returning from the wedding, I received my first Red Cross deployment to Florida, the year of the hurricanes.. I was amazingly calm and made the necessary arrangements and packed. I studied materials on the airplane. The Atlanta flight was delayed. Arrived in Tampa at 2:30 a.m.!! Boy, oh boy, did I grow and amazingly discovered my hesitations were no different than most well-adjusted women my age. If there were no other Red Cross volunteers waiting you were suppose to rent a car and then wait for three others to join you. You've got to be kidding...rent a car?...me? I prayed not to be the first one and not to be the one to drive. I was not the first one...thank-you Lord.

The next four weeks I was so busy my mind had a vacation from my personal problems. Compared to all of these people suffering from the devastation of a hurricane, my lot in life looked pretty cushy. Everyone had to take a computer class for interviewing clients (I was barely computer literate). The joke to my children was that a week later I was asked to teach someone else the class, ha,ha. It took several days to be assigned to an area and then due to a chain of events I ended up being the *driver* for my supervisor who did not like to drive. Well, of course I did it. On my day off I boldly took the city bus to the coast. Marie was shocked. The most exhilarating sight occurred as I gazed out over the water. A water spout formed, came down and touched the water, and then was taken back up and disintegrated. It felt like the hand of God had briefly made itself known. I was feeling alive inside! I did find out Frederick went to Germany with his brother. A Germany trip was always discussed as a trip *we* would take some day but of course it never materialized. The deployment was a wonderful experience and I recommend it to everyone looking for something meaningful to do. Ha, even had my picture in the local paper after returning from the deployment.

Back home I was asked to teach classes now that I had some experience and found out I really enjoyed teaching the Red Cross classes so I also took an actual teaching course. A couple of years later the CPR/First Aid teaching course was offered free of charge. I took it. I am still very nervous before getting in front of a group but once I start I am fine and love it. These things would never have happened when I lived as a codependent of abuse. I was also sent to Florida after Katrina and ended up teaching (I was sure someone more experienced would have risen to the request but *not*) some 400 people who were then sent to Louisiana. Oh, yes, I also drove on that deployment.

In April, 2004, Frederick put on the cloak of pastor when communicating with me. Everything he communicated was the same but delivered in a very professional manner and signed "Pastor". To me it was a cloak of arrogance and deceit, elevating himself above a mere husband and using *Pastor* as a symbol of truthfulness. It made my blood curdle and my stomach nauseous. I had evil thoughts and uttered many out loud. Pastors in the area I left all sided with Frederick and insisted the only resolution to this conflict was for me to come home. No one offered any concern for what may have led to my departure. There was no effort to set up a formal meeting and discuss my ever growing sin of separation. I felt like a bunny being chased by a pack of angry wolves. I received emails from Frederick threatening disciplinary proceedings from the church if I did not return soon. So, it would seem that none of these pastors is interested in possible abuse, sexual immorality, denial of sexual intimacy, and refusal to support me, but only in the fact that I had separated. It would also seem that none of these pastors had contacted previous counselors and for sure they had not contacted Pastor S.

> Turn to me and have mercy on me, for I am alone and in deep
> distress. My problems go from bad to worse. Oh, save me from
> them all! Feel my pain and see my trouble. Forgive all my sins.
> See how many enemies I have, and how viciously they hate

me! Protect me! Rescue my life from them! Do not let me be disgraced, for I trust in you. May integrity and honesty protect me, for I put my hope in you.

Psalm 25:16

The idea of church discipline just became a cloud over my head. I didn't even think about excommunication as the word was never used. And since Frederick was the key player in all of this, I thought he was alone in pursuing this until Pastor S. became aggressive in finding out what was going on. I knew there was no conformity on issues of abuse and sexual immorality. I studied I Corinthians 7 and consulted Pastor S. on the issue of separation. There were opposing views on this as well.

As issues became more heated Pastor S. thought it best if I refrained temporarily from taking communion. That hurt! Pastor S. consulted with his district president and was told to ignore any threats of church discipline coming from Frederick.

The letter of February 14th, 2005, I believe is the first mention of excommunication. At this time nothing was said about anyone from the congregation or other pastors talking to me but just that I should see a former counselor (I never did understand the intent of that letter). Months go by with all these repetitive warnings and the urgency really did not materialize. I had a 'home' church, a caring spiritual leader, and the rest just seemed an endless floundering attempt by Frederick to get rid of me to save his ministry.

During the time lapse my attorney finally put together a settlement proposal. Knowing most of the monies would come from Edward Jones I called them once to find out the status. Our stock investments had increased by $10,000. Edward Jones alerted Frederick that I had called them making inquiries. My attorney checked into Frederick's bank account and found out there was a decrease of $10,000 there. He called Frederick. Frederick indicated he had unusual expenses. After the settlement was final I found out he had bought another Mercedes.

Meanwhile, as requested by Pastor S., I gathered emails and made a time frame of events. Pastor S. informed me that Frederick had called again to check on my status as a church member and asked if I was taking communion. Frederick then called his district president who called my district president who called my area circuit pastor and a meeting was set up with Pastor S. and the assistant pastor. During the meeting Frederick called me to inquire why I checked with Edward Jones and was quick to inform me that since my inquiry stocks had "taken quite a beating." Later I had a meeting with the circuit pastor and once again had to dredge up the past. On the plus side, the circuit pastor had actually taken a class on abuse. He felt that until the situation was settled Frederick should not take communion either.

All of this prompted my attorney to bring a conclusion to the settlement. In the proposal he sent he suggested I would undergo an earning capability test that could be used in court. The one time settlement was by far a better deal for Frederick especially if we were not going to reunite. It had now been a year since this process began. Anger and resentment once again crept into my thoughts. I prayed for these sinful thoughts to be taken away which they were. I knew I had to fully place my trust in the Lord and not in men. Frederick finally agreed and I settled for less than a jury would have accorded me but I just wanted it to be over. What I did receive was to me a lot of money having never been involved with the marital finances nor the freedom to spend any of it. I also made my first big blunder having very little financial knowledge. Either my attorney or the investment agency could have prevented it but neither thought to inform me. I understood the transfer of marital monies would not be taxed. I did not understand transferring them immediately to another institution left me exposed to taxation. Whoops! Since the monies were still in Frederick's name when it transpired he was quick to inform me I owed him the losses that my financial irresponsibility had incurred.

Then started the new warnings that separation was tantamount to divorce and therefore he filed for divorce. At least the decision was not left up to me. I have no idea to this day if I would have followed through with a divorce. The big question in my mind was why there was no intervention on Frederick filing for a divorce. The same passage in I Corinthians 7 that deals with separation clearly states that the man shall not divorce his wife. The divorce was final May 31st. I experienced a short surge of elation but then a melancholy mood descended on me. Was there really no other choice? Did this have to happen? I had no desire to call anyone with the news.

At this time the lady whose apartment I was using received a call and moved out leaving me the apartment and a place to put my soon-to-be-acquired possessions. My sister-in-law and employer/friend agreed to help me retrieve my possessions as they were listed in the settlement agreement. The next weekend we were on our way. I was surprised that their knowledge on renting trailers and making this all happen was no greater than mine. Of course I still assumed I was more inadequate and dumber than most women. Recovery was still happening. What fun we had! So many times I imagined Frederick upset at little mistakes and bad choices but the three of us just kept on a truckin' doing the best we could. I had received emails from Frederick that he would be setting up the times and conditions under which we would be allowed in the house to retrieve my belongings. I chose not to communicate with him. Anyway, we obtained the trailer and went to the house. He was not there. I could feel the fear creeping back into my system so I had my friend call him at his office. He wanted to talk to me but my friend, as instructed, said she was the communications director. Well, he came over, even offered us lunch (we had brought groceries) and was actually helpful as we flew into action. We definitely overwhelmed him and three against one put him ill at ease which gave me strength. At 10:00 p.m. he asked how much longer we were going to work. I said until we dropped and then we would just sleep in the back bedrooms so we could go at it again in the morning. He then demonstrated to my companions his anger in a small way, telling us there was no way I should expect to stay in the house. I did not belong there anymore! But, I reasoned, it wasn't by choice that I was the one who had to leave. It was I who had to spend the money to retrieve my belongings. Why should I rack up another hotel bill? My sister-in-law retaliated mildly (she is capable of much more) and my husband went to bed in a huff! We stayed. Partly his outburst was because he did not want us there in the morning when he had to be at church. He actually asked me not to attend church so as not to make people (him?) uncomfortable. Do you see the hypocrisy of this? A pastor asks a Christian not to attend church and then later puts her under church discipline for being an impenitent sinner.

We got up early and flew into action with minds set to get out of there faster than originally planned. Witnessing the reaction of my friend and sister-in-law was another reality check for me. I did see things clearly. I was not given to over-reactions or misjudging Frederick's outbursts. We loaded what we could but ran out of room before I had everything the judge was allowing me. It was emotionally difficult but at least I felt I had some of my life back. We treated ourselves to a nice hotel where we could calm down and relax. Many times we had to remind ourselves God was in charge and our anger served no purpose. For fun on the way home we stopped at a river casino for an hour. I made $20…a royal straight flush…hurrah!

One month later I receive a notice of excommunication inviting me to appear before the assembly or send a written statement if I so desired. This was four and a half months after the first mention of excommunication. I am shocked and paralyzed! I see pastor S. as soon as possible. He is amazed also that this could happen outside the perimeters set by the church body. He decides to consult the district praesidium and they side with him that this procedure is entirely out of order. For one thing, I am to be given proper notification (priority mail) within a time frame that I am able to make a personal appearance before the church issuing the proclamation. This is note-worthy as these talks had already begun when I retrieved my belongings and Frederick asked me not to attend church. I did write a brief letter (July, 2005) as follows:

Dear Members;

I stand before you, a sinner. I believe in Jesus Christ as my Savior who led a perfect life for me and died on the cross for all of my sins. Heaven is therefore mine. I have no doubts about this!

I do not, however, believe I am living in sin having left my husband. My spiritual life was at stake, not to mention my physical and emotional well-being due to unloving acts, verbal abuse, and the threat of physical abuse. The man, serving as your pastor, was dragging me into the depths of despair…a despair which had become all too common over twenty-seven years of marriage. It was becoming impossible to hear him talk of the love of Christ and then have that same love nonexistent in our daily lives.

If a spouse is an unbeliever one should remain in hopes of bringing him to Christianity. But if her husband is a Christian, incapable of showing the love God requires in a marriage, there is only despair. A contrite heart is demonstrated in a life of change – a new life dedicated to following God's commands. This attitude did not exist.

I do not know at what point I would have actually filed for divorce. I filed for legal separation because all joint marital monies had been cut off from me…another act of lovelessness. It was your pastor who filed for divorce. I held on to a hope and prayed thusly over the twenty-seven years of our marriage that he would truly repent of his sins against me and love me.

Do what you must – to be mistakenly excommunicated from an earthly church body does not sever me from being a member of the one Holy Christian Church on earth. God shall deliver me and I will glorify him!

Your Sister in Christ

Frederick immediately fires back with a professional letter from himself claiming my statements and seemingly supportive bible passages are inadequate and declare no cause for my leaving the marriage. I had another pastor, a relative, read the letter and he is beyond shocked that this could take place and cites many areas where this procedure is unconstitutional (church constitution). Somewhere in all this I talk to an elder in Frederick's congregation, but he will not discuss it. The men in Frederick's church are not strong. It is understandable to me that they are easily led by Frederick who is very controlling.

I decided to find out myself the results of the July 17th meeting. I was told by the president of the congregation that the vote to excommunicate was not obtained (requires a unanimous vote). I did not anticipate how relieved I was going to feel hearing this. But, no, it isn't over… Frederick plans on visiting the dissenting and abstaining votes and having a revote! This was told me by the congregational chairman. This procedure is unheard of! All I received for notification of this next meeting was an incidental e-mail two days before the meeting! .

Again, not wanting to wait, I called the congregational chairman and was informed that though some members did not even attend the meeting and still others abstained from voting, the vote to excommunicate was obtained. He stated he wished he had never been a part of this and would have resigned as chairman if he had known all that was to happen. I assured him I did not hold him responsible for the church letters and laughingly, he assured me there was no way he wrote them. I did not know until I received the letter informing me of the excommunication (not sent priority mail and no information on appeals enclosed) that the reason had been changed from divorce (which Frederick considered equal to legal separation) to separation. Delving once again into the past has been an arduous and painful task but I hope it serves a purpose in helping not just me but others in similar situations.

I received formal notice of the excommunication on a Saturday via regular mail. I proceeded through my day in somewhat of a trance. This just doesn't register as possible. Sunday it hits me. After church I call a friend and end up at her house. She immediately becomes unglued as does her husband. Soon my counselor friend joins us and their mission becomes calming me down and getting food into me. Monday a.m. a seemingly normal itch on one foot ends up being an unscratchable case of itching on all four extremities. I take myself to the emergency room a block away. Eventually I receive a shot of Benadryl and it subsides. Now I must include on health forms that I am allergic to excommunication.

> Be pleased, O God, to deliver me! O Lord, make haste to help me! Let them be put to shame and confusion who seek my life! Let them be turned back and brought to dishonor who desire my hurt! Let them be appalled because of their shame who say, "Aha, Aha!' May all who seek thee rejoice and be glad in thee! May those who love thy salvation say evermore, "God is great!" But I am poor and needy; hasten to me, O God! Thou art my help and my deliverer; O Lord, do not tarry!
>
> Psalm 70

I met with Pastor S. again and it was resolved that I should appeal, a move that rarely happens with lay people. I gathered pertinent correspondence I had had with Frederick. Pastor S. suggested I write a timeline of abuse throughout my marriage and that I appeal to friends and family for letters of facts, as they encountered them with my marriage, to be sent to the appeals committee. Again, it was most difficult emotionally to dredge up the past. I prayed constantly that the Lord keep my anxiety in check so I could concentrate on putting down the chain of events relating to the church discipline noting the lack of scriptural application and church protocol. In spite of all the feelings and issues with Frederick I did consider him above average intelligence but had to remember all of the latest may have been out of desperation and even cunningness to cover up and appear righteous or at least more righteous than me.

> Vindicate me, O Lord, for I have walked in my integrity, and I have trusted in the Lord without wavering. Prove me, O Lord, and try me; test my heart and my mind. For thy steadfast love is before my eyes, and I walk in faithfulness to thee....I wash my hands in innocence, and go about thy altar, O Lord, singing aloud a song of thanksgiving.......My foot stands on level ground; in the great congregation I will bless the Lord.

> Psalm 26:1-3, 6-7, 12

Pastor S. also sent a letter...excerpts as follows;

> Early in Anya's contact with our church she shared with members of our staff the fact she had separated from her husband. She gave some general reasons why – physical and verbal abuse, poor communication, lack of intimacy, and struggles with the fact that her husband, with whom she was having problems, was also her pastor. Anya indicated that she and her husband had varied counseling experiences that seemed to result in little or no improvement in the marriage.

> Our staff gently questioned her about these issues to determine whether Anya had grounds for leaving her husband or not. Anya maintained that she had grounds for separating from her husband but had not ruled out reconciliation if Frederick was willing to substantively address issues of concern. At that time Anya confessed and expressed sorrow over sins she committed in the marriage. She confessed faith in Jesus. From the time Anya came to us her life has been a clear and positive witness of her Christian faith.

> We discussed our concerns with Frederick but he maintained things weren't that bad. We talked to the circuit pastor who

had worked with Frederick and Anya on a limited basis. He indicated this was difficult because it was a "he-said-she-said situation" and involved considerable distance. While the circuit pastor said he didn't know exactly what the situation was, he felt that Anya didn't have grounds to leave Frederick. We shared with him our concern that things were worse than Anya had told him or Frederick would admit.

In June of 2004 we received a letter from Frederick that his church had put Anya under church discipline and asked us to honor it. Our staff replied that if it was Frederick leading the congregation in the discipline process, we would find it difficult to honor the discipline. Our Board of Elders concurred. We again contacted the circuit pastor. We encouraged him to ask Frederick to step aside in this discipline matter. We requested the circuit pastor to take the lead. He replied that the congregation had not asked this of him nor had the district president directed it, so he couldn't do it. He indicated that we should address the matter with the district president.

In August, 2004, I spoke to the district president in person. I inquired whether he knew that Anya maintained that Frederick had abused and abandoned her. He was aware of some of the problems but didn't think them to be that bad. I asked him to direct Frederick to step aside from leading his congregation in disciplining Anya. He refused and told me that if Anya didn't like Frederick's role in her discipline, she could appeal it. We know and respect the district president for his ministry and his strong leadership. We believe, however, that allowing Frederick to direct the discipline of his wife was not a good decision. There are too many issues that could cloud Frederick's perception and objectivity in this discipline process. We understand that there are distance challenges for your district in dealing with this situation. But in a weighty matter such as an excommunication it seems that 'going the extra mile' is in place.

Another concern we have relates to the question, "What constitutes abuse?" Our local Christian Family Counselor worked with Anya. He believes that Anya's description of what she experienced at her home is both abuse and abandonment.

137

Our ministry staff agrees with his understanding of abuse and abandonment. So do our elders. Our concern over abuse has been strengthened as a result of statements from Anya's son Paul. After a Bible Information Class I was doing with him and his wife, he, unsolicited, shared his concern for his mother and father. He lamented his dad's leading his congregation in the discipline of Anya. Then he went on to say that he didn't understand how his dad could be a nice guy to other people, but not to Anya. He indicated that this has been the case for a long time. He believed his dad had abandoned his mother before Anya ever left.

Our final concern revolves around the following issue. Frederick adamantly maintains he isn't guilty of abuse and Anya adamantly claims he is. But humanly speaking no one else knows for sure what happened between them. How then can Frederick's congregation be sufficiently sure Anya didn't have biblical grounds for leaving Frederick and, therefore, isn't impenitent? For this reason and those above we encourage your committee to overturn Anya's excommunication.

We pray for you and ask God's blessings on you and your deliberations.

Waiting was stressful but finally I received a letter declaring my case of excommunication overturned. I was ecstatic. The letter was short and to the point. Frederick sent a letter to the appeals committee declaring they would go through the procedure again adhering to the correct procedures as it was not for spiritual reasons the excommunication was overturned. I could not believe it. Another day with friends calming me and supporting me. However, soon after, I received another more detailed letter that was sent to Frederick stating in no uncertain terms that the excommunication was unspiritual. Hallelujah! It helped to have an attorney on the appeals committee who disagreed with the idea that legal separation was paramount to divorce. Still, no one dealt with Frederick for serving papers of divorce.

I will extol thee, Lord, for thou hast drawn me up, and hast not let my foes rejoice over me. O Lord my God, I cried to thee for help, and thou hast healed me. Thou hast turned for me my mourning into dancing; thou hast loosed my sackcloth and girded me with gladness, that my soul may praise thee and not be silent. O Lord my God, I will give thanks to thee forever.

Psalm 30:1-2, 11-12

My children's support during these days was a tremendous boost. However, we did have some family trials which temporarily took my mind off my own problems. Two of the boys had encounters with the law and we all learned about the judicial system. Thankfully the Lord is ultimately in charge. I had to pray extra hard for several whose faith was being tested. One marriage had major problems. Another opportunity for prayer. One daughter stayed with me awhile…350 square feet is not enough room. She soon made other arrangements. Working together at the Tea Room was exciting short term…long term not good. Understanding and accepting my *situation* was more difficult for one daughter but we finally made a breakthrough and all was well. So there were times when it seemed the Lord was giving me more than I could bear. But trust the sun will shine again and trials will make you stronger. The joy of two grandchildren will quickly dispel all sorrow.

The church discipline issue continued to rear its ugly head. Frederick's congregation refused to release my membership. I received a copy of a letter from Frederick's district president giving them alternatives for further excommunication procedures. Pastor S. is visibly upset when I show him the letters. He talks with his staff and the circuit pastor. He continues to give me communion. He finds out Frederick's district president has referred the case to his first vice president. Eventually Pastor S. calls this pastor and lets him know nothing will change my church status in his mind. The first vice president concedes that he has no intention of proceeding with any further action.

The first year I had many nightmares depicting abuse and an inability to escape. I prayed that God would remove these and He did. I also had to ask for help to keep evil thoughts toward Frederick out of my head during the day. Recovery takes time. I do not know how it can take place without faith and prayer. I continued to have positive relationships with my children. I was able to visit them without the constraints I formerly had from Frederick. Besides walking I went swimming and used a cardiac bike I had acquired from the give- away room at my apartment complex. It was not easy cooking for myself but with encouragement from my children I bought healthier foods.

I have a very strict budget that I stick to and I have never wanted for food, clothing or a roof over my head. I learned quickly that money means very little and living each day to its fullest is what counts.

I have also had many experiences that again would not have happened before I severed myself from the situation that was slowly killing my spirit. My daughter, Marie, loved to travel. I felt obligated to check on her and make sure she was alright. This meant a trip to Boston and another to Hawaii. My son, Paul, lived in Mexico for a couple of years. Of course I had to see my granddaughter! My daughter, Joanne, and family lived different places in Wisconsin. I was able to visit them more often. My son, Michael, flew me to Seattle for a visit. I had a cousin in Washington D.C. whom I stayed with a week while her husband was gone. Her emotional instabilities required a companion. She showed me the sights. What a great experience!

Paul and his family moved back to the United States from Mexico and settled in Dallas where he was able to procure a high school teaching position using his Spanish. He was able to take courses on line to acquire his teaching credentials. I was down there as soon as possible to meet my grandson who had been born in Mexico and of course reacquaint myself with my beautiful granddaughter.

I feel it necessary to make a political statement here. My son, being of above average intelligence and a United States citizen, spent untold hours and money obtaining a visa for his wife and acknowledgement that his son was indeed a U.S. citizen. Even so he had to use his brother, with his law knowledge and peers, to help him through the endless red tape. Every step required an additional fee. His wife's work visa took more time. Perhaps there is a good reason we have so many illegal aliens!

I also became involved in teaching bridge and playing competition bridge with my friend Elaine. I finally finished square dancing lessons and have a dress (very important)! I volunteered to visit people in church. I also started a church newsletter column highlighting a new person/family each month. I once again was proactive in selling my grade school spelling series. I started computerizing pictures with bible passages inserted. I learned to do my own income tax on line. Yes, there were still many lonely hours but for me that really wasn't a change. I lived my married life being lonely especially after the children had grown and left.

I kept in close touch with my children and was able to pray for them instead of listening to Frederick rave about their faults and stupid choices. At first Frederick did not even try to reach out for a positive relationship with his children. However, after a couple of years he increased his visits to them and the time he spent with them. My daughter, Marie, called me after one of these visits and asked, "What happened to my father; has someone taken him?" Her amazement was due to him taking an interest in what she was doing. Not long afterwards I received almost the identical call from my daughter, Joanne. Sadly after a couple years he reverted to his previous demeanor. I am very proud of my children's attitude of taking him for what he is. They understand what he does give is all he is capable of doing.

As a pastor's wife my source of spiritual growth was from my husband. How long do you think someone can be fed from someone who lives a life as described above? Is it a matter of deciding whether there is truth behind these issues and that they exist among us or taking some aggressive action to right the wrong and turn the tide? Now that I've put this down in writing I am not so shocked at the procedures I have endured from the earthly church over the years. The church has chosen the path of least resistance. Embarrassment over the sins of the "brotherhood" wins over love for the souls in danger.

My youngest daughter and family were closest to me. First they were eight hours away, then six, then five and then less than four…Hurrah! They were always looking for advancing a career in organic farming. The last move looked so promising they decided to purchase their first home. My daughter thought I should move into their house. We had many talks. I firmly believed parent(s) should not live with their children. We covered expectations, needing our own space, shared costs…everything we could think of and decided it would work. Offhandedly I emailed all of the children saying how wonderful it would be for all of us to get together and help the mom move. Of course I had been trying for years to get us together and to this end deposited ten dollars into my savings for every birthday and anniversary. Much to my surprise I started receiving affirmations of intent to move me. This was the first time we were all together in over five years. The two sets of grandchildren had never met. It was too wonderful for words. There was a slight damper, however. Prior to moving there was an email concerning some details of the reunion and I happened to notice it was also sent to Frederick. I had to push but finally Marie confessed that, yes, her father was coming. He had not actually been invited but no one tried to hide the fact we would all be together over Thanksgiving. But he would only be there a couple of days so I prayed and got over it and was thankful for at least some time without him. The first ones arrived on Sunday and the last ones on Wednesday. I was with two children on Wednesday. During their conversation Frederick was casually referred to as coming the next day. "No", I exclaimed," you said he was coming Friday." When they confirmed his arrival to be the next afternoon I crashed emotionally. After my alone time and a good cry they both hugged me and told me they would do everything to make me comfortable. In fact it was decided we would have Thanksgiving dinner early with my salmon I caught in Alaska.

I was extremely uncomfortable when Frederick arrived. But shortly after, Thomas and son-in-law asked me if I wanted to come over to the apartment (they had not moved out yet) while they cooked. I didn't catch on at first but finally the looks they were giving me registered…it was an opportunity to get away from Frederick. Over at the apartment the conversation entailed the reasons as to why Frederick chose to come. It was not long after that Frederick came over to the apartment…that gave credence to him coming to actually see me or to be the spoiler. Joanne's husband saved the afternoon by suggesting too many people in the small kitchen would only delay supper.

Back over at the house for supper Frederick led the conversations. I melted into my corner. Thomas did make a point of thanking me for bringing everyone together. After the apartment dwellers left for the night the remaining house group returned to the whys of Frederick's presence. I was obviously not happy about the reunion I had looked forward to for so long. My daughter-in-law looked me in the eye and without reservation told me to quit hanging my head down and allowing him to run things. It was my reunion and I needed to take charge. He could not harm me. Wow! I perked right up and slept well. The next morning I held my head high and from then on executed the plans we had discussed. Amazingly, Frederick melted into the background. It made me wonder if the marriage would have been different had I more frequently taken a stand. But no sense looking back and guessing…one of the rules for recovery. Before everyone left they pitched in to prepare the basement as living quarters for the mom. It was obvious immediately that the noise from upstairs was going to be a problem. Ultimately this did become my number one discomfort. But I was only there for two months before I returned to Alaska.

In April I took a tour from Washington to Texas to Arkansas to Minnesota visiting each of my children. The airfare for all of this was cheaper than a roundtrip to any one of these places…amazing! A highlight of these visits was attending a concert in Eureka Springs, Arkansas. My son, Thomas, was a part of it as a tenor. It was magnificent. It must be told that this group was going to sing at Carnegie Hall. I was already to buy a Carnegie Hall dress but Thomas informed me he wasn't going. The cost was not justified just so one could say he sang at Carnegie Hall. Oh well. I spent a couple weeks at my place in Minnesota. The noise upstairs was bothersome. Joanne made a couple of side comments that were discouraging as far as me making this my permanent abode. On the way to catch a shuttle she came right out and said perhaps I should consider living in Alaska for awhile since I could earn money there. This hurt and I wrestled with my feelings on the long flight to Alaska. I prayed. As we were coming into Anchorage my mood lightened…I felt like I was coming home.

It was almost the end of May and my landlady needed to know if I wanted the room full time otherwise she was going to find a full time border. She hoped I would stay. I prayed. I weighed all of the pros and cons, one con being money. It was definitely borderline whether I could afford it. I decided to trust the Lord on the money and said I would stay. It has been two years and I have always had enough money. Thank-you Lord. I hold nothing against my daughter. I would never have made the move on my own from my apartment in Minnesota. The interim move to my daughter's was merely a stepping stone the Lord provided me so I could easily transition to Alaska. Most of my belongings would remain behind packed and stored with Joanne.

> The steadfast love of the Lord never ceases, his mercies never
> come to an end; they are new every morning; great is they

faithfulness. "The Lord is my portion," says my soul, "therefore I will hope in him." The Lord is good to those who wait for him, to the soul that seeks him. It is good that one should wait quietly for the salvation of the Lord.

Lamentations 3:22-26

DOMESTIC VIOLENCE
abuse

This is a faithful saying, and worthy of all acceptation,
That Christ Jesus came into the world to save sinners,
of whom I am chief.

I Timothy 1:15

This has not meant to be a self-righteous account of my spouse's sins. We all sin on a daily basis. I have been told that part of a twelve step recovery program is to confess all of your sins to another person. I wouldn't know where to start and sorry to disappoint you but I am not even going to try. But I will tell you the specific sins against God's institution of marriage. Co-dependency is reacting to sins in a sinful manner. That is what the abused must guard against.

I would like to first address what I should not have done. I should not have nourished self-pity. Oh, I prayed but when you are fed a steady diet of negative and unloving remarks and actions, well, being a sinful human being aided by a tireless working devil, one has the odds stacked up against being pure of heart. Once filled with self-pity it is easy to take the next step of condoning your own sinful anger and negative comebacks. If you get by with it, it feels good, I mean really good! I was drowning in my sins. I even felt righteous in my anger. Thoughts are as sinful as actions and I had all of them. I was so resentful and filled with self-pity so much of our twenty-seven years together I frequently was unable to have feelings of love and compassion toward my adversary, my enemy, who was supposed to be my loving husband.

However, these are not the greatest sins. The greatest sin of the abused is not looking outside of oneself through the eyes of Christ to the weak faith of the abuser that permits these continuous misguided words and actions. Matthew 18:15 tells us; "If your brother sins against you, go and tell him his fault, between you and him alone." This is what we do as Christians. We keep each other from straying lest our faith grows weak. Telling an abuser he has sinned may very well get you smacked again or endure another tirade but for this remember God will not allow more than you can bear. It would be safe to say this scriptural admonishment won't work. Next Matthew 18:16 says; "But if he does not listen, take one or two others along with you, that every word may be confirmed by the evidence of two or three witnesses." For me this would have been elders in the church or another pastor.

Take a look at the book cover. Which position do you find yourself in? It is possible to raise yourself to the next level on your own. You need to practice seeing yourself as a formidable human being not better than anyone else but not lesser than anyone else. I do not know much advice to give you if you are not a Christian except now would be a good time to find a church and start with a pastor to talk with. Faith, hope and love will begin to raise you up from the fetal and victim positions.

Abusers have many similarities. Many times it is something in their past that has triggered emotional and physical abuse towards you. Christians especially are not happy with the side of them that hurts and injures. Very few will accept counseling. Their low self esteem lives off of their negative controlling. Take that away and who are they? But that is exactly what must be done. Many will never take this step. Meanwhile, seek counseling for yourself. Often this will not be hard to get past your spouse as he insists you are to blame for the problems anyway. So admit you are the problem and get counseling. Some pastors have taken training but usually not. You need to find a Christian counselor that works for you. That means don't settle for the first one if the session doesn't go well for whatever reason.

There is a difference between being persecuted for Christ just because we are Christians and allowing ourselves to be harmed as a result of someone's willful sinning against God's commandments. Is it wrong to take ourselves out of harm's way? Indeed removing one's self is also preventing the abuser from sinning. "Make no friendship with a man given to anger…lest you learn his ways and entangle yourself in a snare." (Proverbs 22:24-25)

Let's begin by defining abuse. Abuse is the misuse of authority; to speak insultingly, harshly, or unjustly; to deceive, berate; to have outbursts of anger; to condemn in an angry hostile way. I believe the key word is anger. "Let every man be quick to hear, slow to speak, slow to anger, for the anger of man does not work the righteousness of God." (James 1:19-20) Anger leads to all of the above which in turn leads to threats or actual acts of physical violence or it can be withholding needs necessary for physical and emotional wellness. "He who forgives an offense seeks love, but he who repeats a matter alienates a friend." (Proverbs 17:9) We are not speaking of everyday sins which we all by our very sinful nature commit. These sins are personal and against what God desires in a marriage. "Love is patient, love is kind. It is not easily angered." (I Corinthians 13:4-5) The sins are malicious and controlling. "An angry man stirs up dissension, and a hot-tempered one commits many sins." (Proverbs 29:22) It is easy to see the extreme; fear of death due to a history of severe beatings. However, this is rare. Most women do not believe their abuser would ever lose control to the point of breaking a bone or seriously injuring her, until they are the one picked up by an ambulance and admitted to the hospital.

Frederick and I did not have a righteous life under God. Devotion and prayer were not a part of our conversation. I'm sorry doesn't mean much when the same display of anger repeats itself over and over and over again. "An ill-tempered man stirs up dissension, but a patient man calms a quarrel." (Proverbs 15:18) Love is a word with little meaning. The abuser becomes defensive and if questioned the fear of being found out only produces more anger. And one sin leads to another. Lying becomes more commonplace, again to cover up other sins.

These sins against marriage vows are often sexual in nature; friendships, ogling, pornography. These will eventually show themselves with changes during sexual intimacy even to the point of total withdrawal. This is covered by Paul in I Corinthians 7:5 "Do not refuse one another except perhaps by agreement for a season, that you may devote yourselves to prayer; but then come together again, lest Satan tempt you through lack of self-control." I have looked back and thought a lot about the parameters of sexual intimacy. It seems the basic commands by God of love and respect would govern any love-making. Sexual intimacy is after all an act of love. How would love be displayed if the object of that love is forced outside of her/his comfort zone? Where would respect be if what pleases one partner is abhorrent to the other? Does leadership under God's command give the husband the right to demand any sexual act? Is a wife under the guidelines of submission required to follow her husband's lead even if the act brings her to tears? I think not! In one counseling session Frederick commented that he wished by this time in our marriage we would have reached a higher plateau in sexual intimacy. I didn't even want to know what plateau he was talking about. Interestingly, this was at the time he no longer engaged with me on any sexual plane. I believe he could no longer find sexual satisfaction due to his escalation in pornography.

The abused feels like a failure. She may doubt her ability to see things clearly, her reality has become skewed, she has guilt from years of being convinced by her abuser that his anger is her fault. Perhaps she should just continue to accept this life of abuse as her trial that God has given her. After all, some hours are good, some days aren't so bad. She often believes that if she just focuses harder on what God expects of her, her desires being to please her husband, and prays for help, she will be okay.

How do we get there? Should we have seen signs while dating? I asked my counselor if I had a sign on my forehead that said I accepted abuse. His answer was only to people who are controllers. You may be able to think of other friends and relatives who always seem to be in charge and you let them! Can we prevent the hole that is dug deeper and deeper? What can we do once we find ourselves codependents of an abusive situation?

I want you to understand I believe marriage is God sanctioned and is forever. I stayed twenty-seven years because I believe this. Therefore I want to address how to keep your marriage but actually make it a marriage. This has to be done early on. The longer you wait the more impossible a positive outcome will be. There are many books written on this subject and I encourage you to read and read and read. You will soon find numerous similarities that victimized women share. You are not alone! You are not alone! You are not alone! I wish I had known this.

Look past the earthly life and pray for your spouse's spiritual life. Remember you are first and foremost concerned with your husband's soul. We have plenty of help from the devil and our sinful flesh to berate our husband. Your goal is to replace your anger, hatred, and self-pity with repentance for these sins and compassion for the abuser. Choose your support group carefully. Most everyone will listen to drama. Choose family/friends who support with God's word rather than just empathize with you or worse, are vociferous against your husband. Do not use your support group as an ear to facilitate your sinful need to run your spouse into the ground. As you rid yourself of anger you will realize he already is the one suffering more than you. Don't seek what you want to hear but what you *need* to hear. We certainly do not need anyone else to commiserate with us in our sinful satisfactions. What we do need is someone who believes us, listens, offers help when and if the time comes to disassociate ourselves from the marriage, and of course takes us repeatedly to God's Word.

If you are able to include your spouse in counseling do not be surprised at his denials and untruths. Depending on how long you have waited to seek outside help, he has practiced his defense mechanisms and will not be broken down easily. Pray for him, pray for patience and pray for your marriage. Do not be surprised that counseling increases his anger. He is not used to a third party interfering with his domain much less siding with his *inferior* wife.

If your counselor recommends separation for a while…do it!! When Frederick and I finally started counseling, in order to maintain control, he went outside of the counselor's recommendations for reading material and found his own which he then read, underlined and passed on to me. All of the underlined applied to me! Your abuser cannot stand the thought that you might be able to function on your own. Remember, he suffers from low self-esteem. You must be lower than him to feed his ego.

Getting away can become an obsession with planning the details over and over in one's mind. It can go on for years because *Fear* keeps it from happening; fear he will come after you and find you and you will see an escalation of anger; fear of people thinking you have a problem (especially when encouraged by your husband, i.e., mental and emotional instability); fear of being shunned by mutual friends, and fear of what the church will do!!!! What if your husband is a called worker, a "man of the cloth"? We all know him, he's a nice guy, he's fun to be around. I've never even heard him raise his voice and if he would she probably deserves it; he's got a great sense of humor; they seem so happy together etc., etc., etc. How quickly we forget to look at ourselves and see the obvious that all of us have our hidden life not exposed to the public eye. No one knows except two people what the intimacies of their marriage relationship are. Why do we kid ourselves that we can determine by observation what the story is? Who of us is so full of wisdom that he can determine from listening to each person's relating of the *Facts* which party is telling the truth? Of course someone experienced and with a gift for counseling should be able to determine some truths.

Only you know the time when the marriage has no hope. No one who has not experienced abuse understands why you stay, why you keep returning. As long as you feel there is a chance you must continue. However, do not stay for the wrong reasons!! God will give you a window of opportunity. He will guide you through your prayer requests. When the door is open have the courage to walk through it. Do not fear the future. Ah, we are back to *Fear*; fear of your husband coming after you, fear of being in charge of your life, fear of being without possessions and/or money, fear of taking care of children alone or not wanting to deprive them of their father, fear of what people will think and fear of the church's response. There are answers to all of these. You are not alone. God will be with you. You may have to move far away. Continue recovery with a group and/or a counselor. Contact those from your support group who offered to help. Reach out! Cry! It is a death but without closure so go through the grieving steps. Take grief counseling. "Humble yourselves, therefore, under God's mighty hand, that he may lift you up in due time. Cast all your anxiety on him because he cares for you." (I Peter 5:6)

While I encourage you take hold of your life and live to the Lord I will never pretend to you that it is easy. But the rewards of not living in fear, of being able to do everyday quotidian as a normal adult, and having normal relationships with family and friends are worth it. The greatest is being at peace with God, not angry, not doubting his promises, but in prayer, thanking and praising him.

I lift my head with shoulders back instead of hanging my head in defeat and waiting for the next confrontation. I am a child of God with gifts and loved not more, not less than anyone else. I make decisions without fear of being reprimanded or put down. I nurture my relationships with my children, grandchildren and friends.

So you have separated. Now what? Hopefully, you left with as much money as you could get your hands on. No hurry but most likely a lawyer will be necessary. Your husband will not go silently into the night. Get rid of the word *fair* as you recover and discover your independence. Life isn't fair. Money and material possessions are not the most important issue. Vengeance belongs to the Lord. The devil, the world and your sinful flesh will tell you otherwise. Don't listen. Do not let yourself be sucked into your spouse's control game. Detach yourself from his sins and weaknesses. Pray, pray and pray!

And do not hang your head in shame. What has happened is not your fault. Abuse is a sin, his sin, not yours. Do not be afraid to open up with people. As Christians we are to share each others' burdens. How are we able to do this if no one knows each others' burdens? Pen a verse describing who you are and where you have come from.

> Mine was:
> I was consumed with grief.
> I called on the Lord for mercy.
> He showed me the way out.
> I am now a recovering co-dependent of an abusive relationship.
> My future is in His hands.
> I am confident He has a purpose for me.
> I will continue to seek wisdom from above.

Shorten it for a simple response. I am a recovering co-dependent of an abusive relationship. You will meet some along the way who have been in your shoes. You will know this immediately by their reaction to your statement. Add them to your support group.

Read over the ten commandments. See which ones you have to particularly be careful of while you become a new person. The devil will be working overtime to turn your recovery into a personal vengeance. Begin journaling as soon as you read this. Record not just facts, but your feelings, your alternatives, and prayers.

Just as no one can give you guidelines when it is time to sever yourself and separate, no one can tell you when and if it is time to divorce. If you decide this is what you must do, please do it with integrity. Do not adopt the possible attitude of your attorney that you should fight for the most you can get. We don't want to act unintelligently about needing support but material gain is not worth an indignant, fist fighting, blood drawing battle. Remember you are a Christian and your actions should reflect this especially to your children. Your words should also reflect your Christian love. Guard yourself that you do not use this time to lash out against your spouse thereby disobeying the eighth commandment. There certainly are

Christian attorneys out there. I wish I had obtained one. If you are cut off from funds you do have the alternative of filing for legal separation thereby obtaining funds without divorce proceedings. It is possible to obtain free legal help but there is usually a long waiting list, mothers of under age children being first on the list.

I'm assuming long before you decided it was time to obtain the services of an attorney you found a pastor who believed your story and is helping you through these rough times. Stand firm! You may have some extremely tough decisions ahead of you. I pray you do not have to decide between leaving your church or undergoing church disciplinary procedures. I hope my battle to stay in my church and appeal my excommunication may lead you to do the same if that is what it comes down to.

Dear Pastors;

The couple sitting in front of you have one thing in common… hopelessness. One does not know how to escape the abuse and the other does not know how to end the cycle of anger and or addiction. Four different Christian counselors suggested separation to me. Why? Because first both need to heal and find answers before they can be together without reacting to each other in a sinful manner. Neither has a handle on reality because they have lived a life of co-dependency. They need to be individually led. "Therefore be clear-minded and self-controlled so that you can pray. Above all, love each other deeply, because love covers over a multitude of sins." (I Peter 4:7-8)

Let's look at I Corinthians7:3: "the husband should give to his wife her conjugal rights, and likewise the wife to her husband." I was denied this but for some reason unbeknownst to me, the topic was never addressed, seemingly cast aside as a rather minor issue. Verses 10 & 11 present a thought unrelated to verses before and after (so a theologian told me). "To the married I give charge, not I but the Lord, that the wife should not separate from her husband but if she does, let her remain single or else be reconciled to her husband - and that the husband should not divorce his wife." "Should not separate" is one phrase of the verse but not the end of the thought. Paul could have left off there but he didn't. It continues; *But if she does...* now we have a major problem....to me it says there is an out but only under conditions where there are no other possibilities seen, when other measures have been exhausted...in other words, a wife living in a co-dependent abusive relationship who has already sought help from counselors. Next problem; how long? I don't mean to make light but you've got to love the choosing of the time duration on this and it is always said with such seriousness that it reeks of legalistic lunacy. A month or two is probably ok, three or four months needs to be looked into as far as the seriousness of this action, five or six months...be careful this is looking like church discipline...seven or eight... this definitely deserves a warning that church discipline is around the corner and on and on and on. If leaving is going to be interpreted as a sin it should be so stated on day one, not some randomly chosen month. What I feel Paul is saying is that sin is lurking after you leave; therefore the initial statement not to leave. And what are the lurking sins? The wife not returning or the husband filing for divorce.

If there is not an agreement among clergy on the practical application of this chapter how can any one lay person be held accountable to the interpretation specifically chosen by the person or persons put in charge of the disciplinary action against this lay person? I would suggest to all lay people that they keep their membership in cyberspace so when an issue arises they will be able to pick in which church/district they prefer to have their case heard. How can I be wrong in how scripture speaks to me if there are learned among us who agree with me? How then can church discipline be brought against me when there is no common stand in regard to what sin I am being charged with and repentance demanded from me?

Recognize you may not be equipped to handle the intricacies of a codependent abusive relationship. People with anger issues are complicated people. They are unable to reconcile their sinful actions with the Christian they profess themselves to be. They must cover up the truth, minimize their sins and yes, even lie. They are incapable of facing the reality of who they have become. They are unable to focus on their spouse and her needs. They are oblivious to their surroundings as it involves the needs of their spouse and what love demands of them. When a presentation or seminar is offered on abuse, pornography etc., accept the invitation and set a date encouraging all men to attend. Those who do not have these sins as part of their lives should be there to support, to encourage, and to understand what is behind these sins.

So is ogling a sin or not? Is there any question about pornography? Shall we continue to make jokes about ogling amongst us, (I have heard many)? Should we continue to deny statistics about the rising internet pornography as far as it infiltrating our church? Or should we help those who have a weakness in regard to this sin? Should we get past the *embarrassment* and consider the souls of these sinners?

Definition of adultery: are we going to narrow this to an *affair* or according to scripture? We know homosexuals have been banned from heaven but I Corinthians 6 also bans the sexually immoral, separately mentioned from adulterers. "Let marriage be held in honor among all, and let the marriage bed be undefiled; for God will judge the immoral and adulterous." (Hebrews 13:4) "But I say to you that everyone who *looks* at a woman lustfully has already committed adultery with her in his heart." (Matthew 5:28) What does Luther say in the meaning to the sixth commandment? Lead a decent life in words and actions and that husband and wife honor and love each other. Is not this about more than just having a sexual encounter outside of the marriage?

If you are a pastor or an elder and a wife comes to you seeking help, try believing everything she says no matter how difficult. Believe me, she probably isn't even telling you everything. Understand how hard it was for her to come to you in the first place. Read books to help your understanding. She doubts whether she should be in your office at all. You cannot imagine the myriad of thoughts that pass through an abused wife's head in one day...from maybe a little bit of medication put into his food or drink each day to calm him down to planning a present or dinner to please him... desperate thoughts of tying him up for a day and doing whatever you want... something causing paralysis so he can't come after you...and yes, running away. Acknowledge the widespread abuse that grows like a cancer in our midst and instead of burying your heads in the sand give counsel to the co-dependents of an abusive relationship. It should not be assumed the woman is spinning an emotional tale of woes and then sent home to be a submissive wife. It should not be assumed the husband is telling the truth when he denies any abuse. Men have their wives at a disadvantage. Pleading a woman's emotional state is often convincing to a pastor who in my circles is a man. This even happens with some experienced male counselors. On the other hand, very few women actually make up stories about abuse. If they were not being abused and wanted to leave the marriage…they would just leave. Also, a small percentage of abused women actually seek out counseling so there are no statistics to base findings on that these women are fabricating the truth of their codependent relations with their abusive husbands.

Should we choose the path of least resistance? Insist the wife honors her marriage, obeys her husband and asks God for help in her trials? Yes, let's ask the *weaker* sex to be submissive but not confront her husband about his sin. Obey but don't be influenced in an ungodly manner by his anger. Respect her husband in spite of his lying and deceitfulness.

What are the margins for abuse? Should she be hit once a year or does it have to be once a month? Does it have to be with a fist or does an open face slap count too? How loud and often does he have to yell to count it as abuse? Does there have to be indecent language with the yelling or not? It has been said to me if my life was not in danger I had no reason to separate. I can't tell you how often I prayed for mercy by having me put out of my misery once and for all. Living in a state of emotional and mental anguish, and spiritual depravation producing physical symptoms certainly is less desirable than death. I also would wake up in a sweat during a recurring dream of my husband dying and me all but dancing on his grave. Forever, these were the only two ways I saw resolve.

Much will be required of you as you have been entrusted to care for the Lord's sheep until His return. Please, I beg you, take a serious look at the details of what constitutes abuse if you have not already done so. Abuse and pornography addiction have invaded our Christian circles big time, and not just lay people!! We, the souls under your care, and our spouses need help. The devil is attacking from all angles. The abused need to be believed and rescued from hopelessness, not just the hopeless state they find themselves in their marriage, but spiritual hopelessness that is overtaking them; this is especially true if they are married to a called worker. Please do not add to their despair by doubting their word, by not wanting to believe such situations exist in our midst.

These men are living in sin. Their sin of abusing and entertaining themselves with pornography are compounded by lying and deceiving. They are in desperate need of the law so they can once again enjoy the peace of the gospel. Please don't turn away from them by seemingly supporting them. Better to save a soul than make a friend. There were many parts of this book that in once again reliving the past, I was brought low. I did not anticipate that the role the church played in my journey would be the hardest to face again. Do not followers of Christ carry each others' burdens? Does this not mean exhorting our brother to save his soul?

How sad even to this day that the *enemies* were leaders in the church. Only one of many asked me to forgive him. So many accusations, so many horrible words pronounced, so much law without gospel, so much against the eighth commandment. Yet only one openly repented, one who needed no forgiveness from me. He fought beside me. He was thrown into the midst of a fire. He was attacked from all directions; twice, not knowing the right path to take, he requested I abstain from communion until such time as there was a more clear understanding. He admits he lost much sleep over this. Given a second chance he would not take that path but having done so he is sincerely sorry. Since there is no such communication from the many others, I have had to work through the hurt and anger on my own. Lord, help me forgive, for without you there is no forgiveness.

While we are on the subject of forgiveness let me surprise you by telling you the easiest person for me to forgive was my abuser because he does not get it. Humanly and earthly speaking he won in so many ways. But spiritually I have no idea where he is at. Since I have received no acknowledgement of his sins and request that I forgive him, I have to assume he still carries them in a cart behind him. He purposely carries them behind him because it is too painful to carry them in front where he would have to look at them. For whatever reasons his inability to love and his need to control prevent him from coming to terms with his sins. And there is no one so far as I know who will in love turn him around and say; it is time to empty this cart, fall down on your knees at the mercy seat of the King of Kings, and beg forgiveness. I have asked all my family and friends to not look with pity on me but send forth prayers to heaven that a *Nathan* be sent to my former abuser.

I pray for all of you who are reading this book because you are living with someone who does not love or respect you. May God give you strength and humility as you make decisions for your future.

> Make haste to answer me, O Lord!
> My spirit fails!
> Hide not thy face from me,
> lest I be like those who go down to the Pit.

Let me hear in the morning of thy steadfast love,
for in thee I put my trust.
Teach me the way I should go,
for to thee I lift up my soul.

Deliver me, O Lord, from my enemies!
I have fled to thee for refuge!
Teach me to do thy will, for thou art my God!
Let they good spirit lead me on a level path!

For thy name's sake, O Lord, preserve my life!
In thy righteousness bring me out of trouble!
And in thy steadfast love cut off my enemies,
and destroy all my adversaries,
for I am thy servant.

Psalm 143:7-12

I have fought the good fight, I have finished the race, I have kept the faith. Henceforth there is laid up for me the crown of righteousness, which the Lord, the righteous judge, will award to me on that Day, and not only to me but also to all who have loved his appearing.

II Timothy 4:7-8

Printed in the United States
By Bookmasters